Segregation
and Desegregation

By T. B. Maston

Christianity and World Issues

Segregation and Desegregation:
A Christian Approach

Segregation
and Desegregation

A CHRISTIAN APPROACH

T. B. Maston

The Macmillan Company · New York · 1959

First Printing

Library of Congress catalog card number: 59-8224

The Macmillan Company, New York
Brett-Macmillan Ltd., Galt, Ontario

Printed in the United States of America

ACKNOWLEDGMENTS

Grateful acknowledgment is made to the publishers
for permission to quote copyrighted material from
the following Biblical translations:

The Macmillan Company, New York, and
Geoffrey Bles, Ltd., London, for THE NEW
TESTAMENT IN MODERN ENGLISH, translated by
J. B. Phillips, copyright 1958 by J. B. Phillips.

Moody Press, Chicago, for THE NEW TESTAMENT,
A TRANSLATION IN THE LANGUAGE OF THE PEOPLE,
translated by Charles B. Williams, copyright
1949 by Moody Press.

The National Council of Churches for the
REVISED STANDARD VERSION of the Bible, copyright
1946, 1952 by the Division of Christian
Education, National Council of the Churches of
Christ in the U.S.A.

TO

the Memory

of

J. HOWARD WILLIAMS

Friend of Man

Prophet of God

Preface

"Racial segregation is a problem of such size and urgency that it dwarfs all other social issues in American life today."[1] It is not only a problem for the South and for the nation; it also has significant international overtones. Furthermore, it is not only a social and political issue but also a major moral and religious issue. The Christian religion, as well as political democracy, has a great deal at stake in the outcome of the present struggle regarding segregation.

In recent years many books have appeared dealing with the contemporary racial situation. Some of these have attempted to analyze the problem, others have given the historic background for the problem, while still others have reported progress regarding it. The present volume does not propose to do any of these things except in a very minor and incidental way. It is primarily an attempt at an evaluation of segregation and desegregation from the Christian perspective. The approach is idealistic in the sense that an effort is made to set out the Christian ideal and to apply that ideal to segregation and desegregation. This is the distinctive emphasis of the book.

The logical place to begin any study of segregation and desegregation is the Supreme Court decision of May 17, 1954. That decision is studied in the first chapter. The following chapter is on the reactions to the decision, with particular emphasis being given to the reactions

[1] The opening sentence of the March, 1957, issue of *Social Progress*, a monthly publication of the Presbyterian Church, U.S.A.

of ministers, church groups, and denominational gatherings. The next two chapters (III and IV) are devoted, in the main, to an attempt to define some terms. This is done because of a conviction that a great deal of misunderstanding and considerable opposition to desegregation stem from a failure to think clearly regarding the real meaning of separation, segregation, desegregation, integration, and intermarriage.

While the entire volume is written from the Christian viewpoint, the Christian emphasis is somewhat restrained in the first half of the book. Beginning with Chapter V, the approach is more specifically Christian. After an examination of segregation in the light of some basic biblical teachings (V) and in relation to the Christian ethic (VI), we turn to the churches and segregation (VII), and finally to the effects of segregation on the world mission enterprise (VIII). There is a brief conclusion (IX).

Many people who are actively involved in the contemporary controversy regarding segregation have never seen the Supreme Court's decision of 1954 and its decree of 1955. Both the decision and the decree are reproduced in the appendices. A brief reading list is also provided, with major emphasis on recent publications, for those who care to do some additional study.

The book has been written largely for general reading. I hope that it will be helpful to Christian laymen, to women, to young people, as well as to ministers. I also trust that those who read it will do so prayerfully, that they will approach its study with a mind that is seeking for the truth and with a heart that will be responsive to the leadership of the Holy Spirit. May all of us seek to know the will of God for our lives in the area of race relations. May we ask him to help us to make our own distinctive contribution to the solution of the acute racial problems of our day. We should pray not only for ourselves but also for all of God's children of every class and color, who are likewise seeking to know and to do his will.

I acknowledge my indebtedness to some busy colleagues who read portions of the manuscript and made helpful suggestions concerning it: L. R. Elliott, Cal Guy, W. Boyd Hunt, and C. W. Scudder.

Special gratitude is expressed to Foy Valentine, friend and fellow worker in the field of applied Christianity, who read the entire manuscript and whose appraisal led to its improvement in many ways. Needless to say, none of these friends is in any way responsible for what is said; that must be my responsibility alone. I express my appreciation to the different secretaries who have worked with me on the manuscript, but particularly to Mrs. Melvin B. Bridgford, who prepared the final typescript. Special thanks are due Charles P. Johnson, the librarian, and the library staff of the Fleming Library of Southwestern Baptist Theological Seminary for many courtesies and for their efficient service.

T. B. MASTON

Contents

I The Supreme Court's Decision   1

Occasion for the Decision   1
Content of the Decision   3
Background for the Decision   7
Atmosphere Favorable for the Decision   12

II Reactions to the Decision   20

Immediate Reactions   20
Resistance to the Decision   24
Reactions of Negroes   28
Reactions of the Churches   31
"The New Reconstruction"   37

III Separation and Segregation   41

Separation Versus Segregation   41
Separation and Segregation   44
Segregation and Discrimination   52
The Cost of Segregation   56

IV Desegregation and Integration   62

Desegregation Versus Integration   62
Desegregation: Progress and Problems   66

Desegregation: Plans and Prospects 70
Integration and Intermarriage 73

V Biblical Teachings and Segregation 81

The Nature of God 82
The Nature of Man 86
The Work of Christ 91
God's Attitude Toward Man 93
Man's Relation to His Fellow Man 97
A Postscript: "The Curse of Ham" 99

VI Segregation and the Christian Ethic 101

The Will of God 101
Perfection 106
Love 109
The Cross 113
The Holy Spirit 117

VII The Church and Segregation 122

"The Church of God" 123
"The Body of Christ" 124
A Fellowship 129
The Churches: An Appraisal 133
The Churches: Their Problems 137

VIII Segregation and World Missions 143

The Commission of the Churches 144
The Peoples of the World 146
The Challenge of Communism 150
The Burden of the Missionaries 154

IX Conclusion: A Statement of Convictions 163

Appendix A 168

United States Supreme Court Decision
(May 17, 1954)

Appendix B 173

United States Supreme Court Action
(May 31, 1955)

Reading List 176

CHAPTER ONE

The Supreme Court's Decision

No phase of the contemporary racial situation can be understood properly without an acquaintance with the United States Supreme Court's decision of May 17, 1954.[1] That decision, which declared that school segregation was contrary to the federal constitution, was one of the most significant and controversial decisions that the Court has ever made. The Court itself evidently sensed the importance of the decision. Justice Robert H. Jackson left a hospital the morning of the decision that all nine justices might be present when the decision was read. In addition, contrary to its usual custom the Court did not give newsmen an advance copy of the opinion. That opinion initiated, and in a sense climaxed, a revolution of major proportions in the social customs and racial patterns of our nation.

For one to discuss intelligently the May, 1954, decision, he must understand the occasion for the decision, its content, and the background for it.

Occasion for the Decision

The Supreme Court, which is the most powerful judicial body in the world and which has the final word concerning the meaning of

[1] A book that deals thoroughly with the decision and its background is the one by Albert P. Blaustein and Clarence Clyde Ferguson entitled *Desegregation and the Law* (New Brunswick, N.J., Rutgers University Press, 1957). The subtitle is "The Meaning and Effect of the School Segregation Cases."

1

the United States Constitution, had before it cases from four states—Kansas, South Carolina, Virginia, and Delaware—and from the District of Columbia. The cases challenged the validity of the separate-but-equal doctrine, which was based on a decision by the Supreme Court in 1896, and which had been accepted generally as the law of the land in the area of race relations.

Previous to 1952 a number of cases had come before the Court requiring interpretation, amplification, and application of the separate-but-equal doctrine. Some of these were in the area of education, mostly on the graduate level. Although these cases required reexamination of the doctrine, they did not directly challenge it. However, as we shall see later, there was a gradual movement toward a frontal attack on the separate-but-equal concept and hence on segregation as such. This movement was climaxed in the McLaurin (Oklahoma) and Sweatt (Texas) cases, which were decided by the Court in 1950.

The challenge of the separate-but-equal doctrine was made definitely and pointedly in the five cases decided by the Supreme Court in 1954. The cases from the four states were so similar that the Court felt justified in handing down a consolidated judgment or opinion. Chief Justice Warren, speaking for the Court, said that although the cases were "premised on different facts and different local conditions," they involved "a common legal question which justified their consideration together." The legal basis for the District of Columbia case was somewhat different. The District is not a state, and hence the "equal protection" clause of the Fourteenth Amendment did not apply. In contrast to the cases from the states, which were premised on the "equal protection" clause, the case from the District of Columbia appealed to the "due process" clause of the Fifth Amendment. This explains the fact that the Court passed on the latter case separately, although at the same time and with the same results as on the cases from the states.

Section I of the Fourteenth Amendment, which includes the "equal protection" clause, reads as follows:

All persons born or naturalized in the United States, and subject to the jurisdiction thereof, are citizens of the United States and of the State wherein they reside. No State shall . . . abridge the privileges or immunities of citizens of the United States; nor shall any State deprive any person of life, liberty, or property, without due process of law, nor deny to any person within its jurisdiction the equal protection of the laws.

The plaintiffs in all cases from the states argued that segregation in the public schools violated the "equal protection" clause. They contended that this clause required equality and hence equal treatment. It was further argued that since segregation inflicts mental harm on Negro children, segregated education was and is inherently inferior and therefore contrary to the "equal protection" provision of the Fourteenth Amendment.

Content of the Decision[2]

The cases were first argued before the Court in its 1952 term. On June 8, 1953, the last day of that term, the Court ordered that the cases be reargued the next fall. The following specific questions were directed to the counsel on both sides:

In their briefs and on oral argument counsel are requested to discuss particularly the following questions insofar as they are relevant to the respective cases:

1. What evidence is there that the Congress which submitted and the State legislatures and conventions which ratified the Fourteenth Amendment contemplated or did not contemplate, understood or did not understand, that it would abolish segregation in the public schools?

2. If neither the Congress in submitting nor the States in ratifying the Fourteenth Amendment understood that compliance with it would require the immediate abolition of segregation in public schools, was it nevertheless the understanding of the framers of the Amendment

(*a*) that future Congresses might in the exercise of their power under Sec. 5 of the Amendment, abolish such segregation, or

(*b*) that it would be within the judicial power, in light of future conditions, to construe the Amendment as abolishing such segregation of its own force?

2 See Appendix A for the text of the decision.

3. On the assumption that the answers to questions 2(a) and (b) do not dispose of the issue, is it within the judicial power, in construing the Amendment, to abolish segregation in public schools?

4. Assuming it is decided that segregation in public schools violates the Fourteenth Amendment

(a) would a decree necessarily follow providing that, within the limits set by normal geographic school districting, Negro children should forthwith be admitted to schools of their choice, or

(b) may this Court, in the exercise of its equity powers, permit an effective gradual adjustment to be brought about from existing segregated systems to a system not based on color distinctions?

5. On the assumption on which questions 4(a) and (b) are based, and assuming further that this Court will exercise its equity powers to the end described in question 4(b),

(a) should this Court formulate detailed decrees in these cases;

(b) if so what specific issues should the decrees reach;

(c) should this Court appoint a special master to hear evidence with a view to recommending specific terms for such decrees;

(d) should this Court remand to the courts of first instance with directions to frame decrees in these cases, and if so, what general directions should the decrees of this Court include and what procedures should the courts of first instance follow in arriving at the specific terms of more detailed decrees?

The Attorney General of the United States is invited to take part in the oral argument and to file an additional brief if he so desires.

The Court in its decision of 1954 said that the reargument of 1953 "was largely devoted to the circumstances surrounding the adoption of the Fourteenth Amendment in 1868." The Court concluded, however, that it could not decide the cases before it merely on the basis of the historic background and interpretation of the Fourteenth Amendment. One difficulty was the status of public education at the time of the amendment's adoption. Since the education of Negroes was almost nonexistent at that time, it was natural that there would be little in the history of the Fourteenth Amendment relative to its intended effect on public education.

The Court further suggested: "We must consider public education in the light of its full development and its present place in American life throughout the Nation. . . . Today, education is

perhaps the most important function of state and local governments.
. . . It is the very foundation of good citizenship." The Court said
that the clock could not be turned back to 1868, when the amendment was adopted, or "even to 1896 when Plessy v. Ferguson was
written." The latter established, on a legal basis, the separate-but-
equal doctrine.

The Court then faced, in its decision, the pointed question: "Does
segregation of children in public schools solely on the basis of race,
even though the physical facilities and other 'tangible' factors may
be equal, deprive the children of the minority group of equal educational opportunities?" They answered their own question by saying, "We believe that it does."

After a brief statement concerning the Sweatt case and the Kansas
case the Court stated its decision as follows: "We conclude that in
the field of public education the doctrine of 'separate but equal' has
no place. Separate educational facilities are inherently unequal." The
Court concluded that the plaintiffs in the cases from the four states,
with "others similarly situated," had been "deprived of the equal
protection of the laws guaranteed by the Fourteenth Amendment."

The vote on the historic decision was unanimous. This meant
that all the justices said the same thing—Republican or Democrat,
Jew or Gentile, Protestant or Catholic, Northerner or Southerner,
liberal or conservative. There was no minority opinion, not a single
dissenting vote, which is unusual in Supreme Court decisions. This
fact was a significant feature of the decision, although some have
wondered if it was "unanimous on purpose." In other words, did
the decision really express the judgment of all nine justices, or did
they conclude that the issue was so explosive that a minority group
agreed to concur with the majority? The latter would seem very
questionable, when we realize the maturity and independence of
the judges and their reputation for personal integrity. In evaluating
the decision it may also be wise to remember that only two of the
justices—Warren and Burton—were Republicans, with three of the
seven Democrats from the South—Black of Alabama, Clark of Texas,
and Reed of Kentucky.

The Court recognized, at least to some degree, the potential problems its decision might create for some areas. For this and possibly for other reasons the cases were restored to the docket, and the parties to the cases were asked to present further arguments "on questions 4 and 5 previously propounded by the Court." In addition to the Attorney General of the United States the attorneys general of the states requiring or permitting racial segregation in public education were invited to present their views. The United States and the following states filed briefs and participated in the oral arguments: Arkansas, Florida, Maryland, North Carolina, Oklahoma, and Texas.

The Supreme Court decided in its May, 1955, action that the implementation of the Court's decision should be supervised by the federal district courts. The Court said that these courts should be guided "by equitable principles," and that "equity has been characterized by a practical flexibility in shaping its remedies and by a facility for adjusting and reconciling public and private needs."

The Court did conclude, however, that "it should go without saying that the vitality of these constitutional principles cannot be allowed to yield simply because of disagreement with them." The Court further decreed:

While giving weight to these public and private considerations, the courts will require that the defendants make a prompt and reasonable start toward full compliance with our May 17, 1954, ruling. Once such a start has been made, the courts may find that additional time is necessary to carry out the ruling in an effective manner. The burden rests upon the defendants to establish that such time is necessary in the public interest and is consistent with good faith compliance at the earliest practicable date.

.   .   .   .

The judgments below . . . are accordingly reversed and the cases are remanded to the District Courts to take such proceedings and enter such orders and decrees consistent with this opinion as are necessary and proper to admit to public schools on a racially nondiscriminatory basis with all deliberate speed the parties to these cases.[3]

[3] See Appendix B for the text of the May, 1955, action of the Supreme Court.

The words "at the earliest practicable date" and "with all deliberate speed" have left the district courts considerable freedom in applying the ruling of the Supreme Court to local communities. The courts have also had considerable liberty in determining whether or not particular programs or plans for compliance are "consistent with good faith." Some plans that have been approved have provided for gradual desegregation, such as those at Austin and San Antonio, which began at the senior high school level and are working down year by year, and at Nashville, Tennessee, which began with the first grade in September, 1957.

The expression "with all deliberate speed"[4] has been somewhat confusing to courts and communities. It sounds, on the surface, contradictory. The phrase directly applied only to the states involved in the original litigation and the District of Columbia. Legally, however, the decision of 1954 and the interpretation and implementation of May, 1955, also applied to all of the seventeen Southern and border states, which at that time required segregated schools, and also to the four states—Arizona, Kansas, New Mexico, and Wyoming— which permitted but did not require the maintenance of separate schools.

Background for the Decision[5]

The historic decision concerning the school segregation cases did not represent a sudden change in the thinking of the Supreme Court. The action had been foreshadowed by previous decisions. It was the logical culmination of concepts which evidently had been maturing for some time in the mind of the Court. It represented the extension of trends—legal, political, social, and religious—that had been going on for some time. "It hastened the march of events

[4] Don Shoemaker of Southern Education Reporting Service has edited a factual type of book that has the title *With All Deliberate Speed* (New York, Harper, 1957). It is on segregation and desegregation in Southern schools. The chapters are by staff members or those who have had close touch with SERS and *Southern School News* published by it.

[5] The first six chapters of Herbert Hill and Jack Greenberg, *Citizen's Guide to Desegregation* (Boston, The Beacon Press, 1955), provide a compact, helpful study of the background of the May, 1954, Supreme Court decision.

by accelerating processes which began long ago."[6] To trace those trends or processes thoroughly one would have to begin with the founding of our nation and the writing of our Constitution. He would have to trace the gradual extension of the rights of citizenship to all the people.

The legal background for the May, 1954, decision goes back at least as far as the Sarah Roberts case in Massachusetts (1850), when the State Supreme Court denied her the privilege of attending a school with white children. The problem has been considered over and over again through the intervening years by state and federal courts. The separate-but-equal concept, which was directly attacked in the cases from the four states, which led to the May, 1954, decision, was not utilized by the majority of the United States Supreme Court in the disposition of any case before Plessy v. Ferguson in 1896. That was a case that was appealed to the Court from Louisiana, and involved transportation. Incidentally, Plessy was only one-eighth Negro. The Court declared at that time that racial segregation laws were valid exercises of the police services of the states and did not imply racial inferiority. It enunciated clearly for the first time, from the legal viewpoint, the separate-but-equal doctrine.

It may be interesting to note that Justice Harlan expressed a dissenting opinion in the Plessy v. Ferguson case and said, among other things, the following: "In my opinion, the judgment this day rendered will, in time, prove to be quite as pernicious as the decision made by this tribunal in the *Dred Scott Case*.[7] . . . The thin disguise of equal accommodations for passengers in railroad coaches will not mislead anyone, nor atone for the wrong this day done."

---

[6] *Psychiatric Aspects of School Desegregation*, p. 8, published by Group for the Advancement of Psychiatry, Report Number 37, 1957.

[7] In the Dred Scott case (1857) the Supreme Court decided that Scott, as a Negro, was not a citizen of the United States within the intent of the Constitution. In a series of personal judgments the Court stated that Negroes had never been recognized in American law or custom as persons, that they were regarded in the Constitution as property, that the words "people" or "citizens" in the Declaration of Independence and in the Constitution did not include or refer to Negroes. The Court further stated that Negroes were "so far inferior that they had no rights which the white man was bound to respect."

After the Plessy v. Ferguson case the separate-but-equal doctrine was applied by the Supreme Court to several school cases. Notable among these was the Gong Lum (a Chinese girl) case from Mississippi (1927). In this case the separate-but-equal concept was treated as being well established.

The Supreme Court considered several educational cases between the Lum case and the 1954 decision. Even a casual acquaintance with these cases would reveal a gradual weakening of the separate-but-equal theory. The courts in general, but the Supreme Court in particular, began "chipping away" at the separate-but-equal doctrine. It is also true that the Court's progressively more stringent interpretation of the "equal" portion of the doctrine kept constant pressure on the regions that practiced segregation. The validity of the theory or doctrine, which was a part of the American caste structure, began to crumble when the courts, but particularly the Supreme Court, began in the 1930's to give preferential treatment to civil rights rather than to property rights.[8]

In the realm of higher education the original "breakthrough" was achieved in 1935 when the courts ordered the University of Maryland to admit a Negro named Donald Murray. In the Gaines case (1938) from Missouri the Supreme Court said that to require a Negro to accept a tuition grant and to go to another state to secure a legal education was a violation of the "equal protection" clause of the Fourteenth Amendment. This was considered true because there was a law school for white students in the state. After the Gaines case other educational cases reached the Supreme Court which whittled away at the separate-but-equal doctrine. The most significant of these cases were the McLaurin (Oklahoma) and the Sweatt (Texas) cases. Both of these cases reached the Supreme Court during the same year, 1950. They were prepared carefully. For example, Sweatt's lawyers directly alleged that segregation in education violated the Constitution. It was the first educational case

---

[8] Morroe Berger in *Equality by Statute* (New York, Columbia University Press, 1950, 1952) has two interesting chapters entitled "The Supreme Court, 1868–1937: Buttressing the Caste Order" and "The Supreme Court, 1937–1950: Undermining the Caste Order."

to reach the Supreme Court that specifically challenged segregation as such. The lawyers also pointed out, as had been done in previous cases, the inequalities of the facilities offered to Sweatt as compared to the law school for white students at the University of Texas. In other words, the lawyers rested their case on the old while at the same time they looked forward to the new. The Court in its decision, which was favorable to Sweatt, gave consideration, for the first time, to intangible as well as tangible factors in determining that the facilities were unequal.

The McLaurin case was as significant as, and possibly more significant than, the Sweatt case. McLaurin sought to enroll for a doctorate in education. After some delay he was admitted to the University of Oklahoma but on a segregated basis. He sat at a segregated desk in the anteroom to the classroom, at a segregated table in the library, and at a segregated seat in the school cafeteria. By the time his case reached the Supreme Court, however, these limitations had been removed. The only distinction was that he sat in an assigned seat in classrooms, while the white students were free to choose their own seats.

The Supreme Court recognized, in its decision on the school segregation cases of May, 1954, the significance and relevance of the Sweatt and McLaurin cases. Regarding the decision of the Court concerning the Sweatt case, the Court in 1954 said that "in finding that a segregated law school for Negroes could not provide them equal educational opportunities, this Court relied in large part on 'those qualities which are incapable of objective measurement but which make for greatness in a law school.' " Some of those qualities specifically mentioned by the Court in the Sweatt decision were: "Reputation of the faculty, experience of the administration, position and influence of the alumni, standing in the community, traditions and prestige."

The Court in its May, 1954, decision also referred to the McLaurin case. It said that in the decision favorable to McLaurin the Court "in requiring that a Negro admitted to a white graduate school be treated like all other students, again resorted to intangible considerations:

' . . . his ability to study, to engage in discussions and exchange views with other students, and, in general, to learn his profession.' " The Court in the 1954 decision then added: "Such considerations apply with added force to children in grade and high schools. To separate them from others of similar age and qualifications solely because of their race generates a feeling of inferiority as to their status in the community that may affect their hearts and minds in a way unlikely ever to be undone."

The relation of the 1954 decision to the Sweatt, McLaurin, and other cases, and to the earlier Plessy case and its separate-but-equal doctrine clearly reveals that the law of the land, and particularly the interpretation of that law, is not static but dynamic. The basic concepts of the law may and do remain unchanged, but the application of those concepts to particular situations definitely changes. This seemingly must be true if the law, as represented by our Constitution, is to meet the challenge of new conditions, if it is to be abidingly relevant. This idea of the dynamic nature of any basic document should not be surprising. It is even true of the Bible. The latter is not a static book. Its fundamental principles are unchanging; they are eternally valid. However, comprehension of those principles and our understanding of their relevance for the problems of our day change or progress. There is a very real sense in which the Bible is a growing book for those who seek to know its truths and attempt to relate those truths to the changing problems and needs of their own lives and to the life of the world.

The justices of the Court recognized that the Constitution and their interpretation of it could not be static. In their May, 1954, decision, they said, "We cannot turn the clock back to 1868 . . . or even to 1896." In other words, new problems and particularly new insights require a new interpretation. As early as 1940 Associate Justice Hugo L. Black had said for the entire Court, "No higher duty, no more solemn responsibility, rests upon this Court, than that of translating into living law and maintaining this constitutional shield deliberately planned and inscribed for the benefit of every human being subject to our Constitution—of whatever race, creed or persuasion." Notice the words "living law." Because of this "living law" concept, and other significant factors, the walls of racial segregation had been crumbling for some time and for the decade preceding 1954 at a constantly accelerating rate.

Atmosphere Favorable for the Decision

There are usually a number of forces or factors that help to explain changing interpretations of any basic document such as the Bible or a political instrument such as the United States Constitution. Why did the Supreme Court approve the separate-but-equal doctrine in 1896 and set it aside in 1954? What led to the different interpretations of the Fourteenth Amendment and particularly its "equal protection" clause? Why did the judges of the Court say in 1954 that separate facilities were inherently inferior—a thing they had definitely not said fifty years before? Why should they give consideration to intangible as well as tangible factors in making their decision? We cannot answer all of these questions, but we shall set forth a few factors that helped to create the climate favorable to the decision, which represented a change in the Court's perspective.

The marked improvement of the educational and cultural level of the American Negro in recent years has contributed to a deepening consciousness of race on his part, to a greater pride in the accomplishments of representatives of his race, and to a more vocal and militant demand for equality of opportunity. One symbol of the educational advance of the Negro is the marked increase in the number of public high schools in the United States for Negroes and in the number enrolled in those schools. One study reveals an increase in Negro school population in thirteen Southern states of only 4.4 per cent from 1900 to 1940. In contrast, the school enrollment of Negroes during the same period increased in those states 56.7 per cent, with a fantastic increase of high school enrollment of 3,412 to 228,077, or a 6684.6 per cent increase.[9] There has also been a sharp increase in the number of Negro college graduates. There were more who graduated in the

[9] Truman M. Pierce, et al., White and Negro Schools in the South: An Analysis of Bi-racial Education (Englewood Cliffs, N.J., Prentice-Hall, 1955), p. 86.

ten-year period from 1926 to 1936 than during the preceding century. By 1940 approximately ten thousand Negroes were receiving bachelor's, master's, or doctor's degrees each year, which was more than had graduated during the first twenty years of the twentieth century.[10] The advance in education provided the Negro people with a better trained and a more skilled leadership. Furthermore, the better trained Negroes were increasingly unwilling to accept a permanently secondary status.

The demand for equality in treatment and opportunity increased considerably during World War II, when the Negro actually had to struggle for the right to fight as an equal for his country. His experiences in the armed services at home and abroad strengthened his conviction that he should have the full privileges of first-class citizenship. He used the war tactically to improve his position. Advances that he made during the war were not surrendered when peace came. It is also true that some of the leadership among white people who sought improved status for Negroes came from men who had rubbed shoulders with the Negro soldier in the camps of this country, and who had fought by his side in Europe or in the Pacific.

In the years immediately preceding the Supreme Court decision, the Negroes had made marked progress along many lines. They had won recognition in all types of athletics, including professional baseball. They were exercising increasing political power. This stemmed, to some degree, from their movement in such large numbers, beginning in the days of World War I, to the industrial centers of the North. They have definitely helped in recent years to shape national politics. They were also gaining increasing political prestige and power in the South. For example, at the time the Court handed down its decree Negroes were serving as members of city councils, school boards, and other governing bodies in a number of Southern cities. The progress that they had made along various lines increased their desire for equality of treatment and tended to make them more vocal in their demands.

[10] Ina Corinne Brown, *The Story of the American Negro* (rev. ed.; New York, Friendship Press, 1950), p. 173.

There had also been for some time a deepening disturbance of the conscience of many of the majority white group. This led them to be more willing to do something about the unequal and unjust treatment of the Negro. This willingness in turn explains the relatively rapid progress in the improvement of the Negro's status, even in the Deep South. In contrast, this disturbance of conscience may help to explain from the psychological viewpoint some of the rather violent emotional reactions to the Supreme Court's decision and the hardening of the resistance to compliance with the Court's order in some sections.

Another factor that helped to create the atmosphere favorable for the Court's decision was the fact that the United States had become a world power. Peoples around the world know and are concerned about what goes on within our country. One of our nation's chief handicaps in world leadership has been its failure to apply consistently democratic principles to its minority groups. Included in the brief the United States filed in the McLaurin and Sweatt cases was a statement concerning the harm that racial segregation does to the United States in foreign relations. The brief said that "racial discrimination, as exemplified by segregation, has been a source of serious embarrassment to this country. It has furnished material for hostile propaganda and raised doubts about our sincerity even among friendly nations." The national government's brief in the school segregation cases quoted the Secretary of State as follows:

International influence

The hostile reaction among normally friendly peoples . . . is growing in alarming proportions. In such countries the view is expressed more and more vocally that the United States is hypocritical in claiming to be the champion of democracy while permitting practices of racial discrimination here in this country.

The segregation of school children on a racial basis is one of the practices in the United States that has been singled out for hostile foreign comment in the United Nations and elsewhere. Other peoples cannot understand how such a practice can exist in a country which professes to be a staunch supporter of freedom, justice, and democracy. The sincerity of the United States in this respect will be judged by its deeds as well as its words.

Racial discrimination in the United States remains a source of constant embarrassment to this government in the day-to-day conduct of its foreign relations; and it jeopardizes the effective maintenance of our moral leadership of the free and democratic nations of the world.

How much effect the statement from the Secretary of State, which included the preceding quotation, had on the Court no one knows. One would judge that it had some effect.

The lawyers of the National Association for the Advancement of Colored People (NAACP) said, "Survival of our country in the present international situation is inevitably tied to the resolution of this domestic issue." The growing awareness by many Americans of the effects of our racial policy on our foreign relations at least helped to create the general atmosphere favorable for the Court's decision.

Communism helped to create the atmosphere that was favorable for the Court's decision, but in a way different from what is sometimes charged. It has challenged and is challenging the United States on every hand. Our failure to apply consistently our democratic principles and Christian teachings to racial minorities at home and to the great racial majority around the world is one of the weakest spots in our American way of life. Communism has called attention to and sought to capitalize on this weakness or failure. The communists have used it rather effectively to challenge our nation for the leadership of the peoples of the world.

Another element of major significance in the changing climate regarding race relations in our country has been the deepening awareness that the world is in a major crisis period. The contemporary crisis or revolution, in a sense, is a revolution of the colored peoples. They have been suppressed for centuries. The inevitable explosion has come. New independent nations have come to birth: India, Pakistan, Iran, Indonesia, Ghana, and others. All over Asia and Africa there is a stirring among the people, a growing sense of independence. Colonial empires are dead or dying. The Court decision of May, 1954, was, in a sense, a symbol of the revolution which marks our times and grips our world.

Many things have contributed to this world crisis, which involves most of the colored peoples of the world. For one thing, those colored peoples have awakened to the fact that they are not a minority but a majority. They are feeling their strength, at least the strength that comes from numbers. Whatever may be the reasons for the movement, the masses are on the move around the world. Our own colored citizens are catching step with those marching masses, whose march or movement seems to be inevitable and irresistible.[11]

One of the reasons for the movement among the masses is the impact of the Christian movement on those masses. There was a time in the past when the underprivileged peoples of the world, many of whom were and are colored, sat at the feet of the white man, more or less as pupils and inferiors. But the Christian gospel, carried to them in the main by the white man, began to take hold among those masses. That gospel says that all men are equal before God, that the heavenly Father is no respecter of persons, that when one becomes a Christian he is a new man or a new creation in Christ Jesus, and that all men are to be treated with equal dignity and respect. These great truths were bound to germinate and ultimately to lead to a demand for equal status among the peoples of the world.

At a time when the masses of the world are stirring, it is possible that what we in the United States do about the men of color in our midst will determine what we shall be able to do for and with the colored peoples of the world. Furthermore, we should remember that these colored masses, who compose approximately three-fourths of the peoples of the world, may determine the destiny of our civilization and of our world.

Another factor of considerable importance in creating the climate favorable to the Supreme Court decision was the advance in certain sciences such as anthropology, sociology, and psychology. The findings of these sciences have helped to dispose of many of the arguments that had been used to justify segregation and discrimination. The progress that had been made in a better understanding of the

[11] See Frank C. Laubach, *Wake Up or Blow Up* ... (Westwood, N.J., Revell, 1951).

races of mankind represents a real revolution in scientific theory, or what has been termed "a scientific landslide."

The findings of the various sciences[12] were used by the plaintiffs in the cases before the Supreme Court from the four states—Kansas, South Carolina, Virginia, and Delaware. A total of more than forty educators and social scientists testified in the cases, all but five or six for the plaintiffs. The testimony of those educators and social scientists filled the better part of four volumes of the testimony that reached the Supreme Court. For the South Carolina, Virginia, and Kansas cases "a joint document was drawn up by some of America's outstanding sociologists, anthropologists, psychologists, and psychiatrists."[13] Hill and Greenberg suggest that "the purpose of this brief was to present to the court in definitive form the thinking of social scientists about segregation and desegregation."[14] The extensive use of specialists and the heavy documentation of the cases, as planned by the staff for the plaintiffs, help to explain the heavy cost of the cases. Whereas it is estimated that it ordinarily costs $50,000 to $100,000 to carry a case through the Supreme Court, the school segregation cases cost approximately $200,000. The multiplicity of cases would also help to explain the cost.

How much the Court was influenced by the testimony and data provided by the scientists cannot be known. Some have charged that it was a psychological and sociological rather than a legal decision. While this is doubtlessly an extreme statement, nevertheless the findings and the testimony of social scientists injected a new element in legal procedure. Nonlegal materials were introduced into a case and were considered and cited in the decision. It seems that the findings of the social scientists provided some of the basis for the heavy con-

[12] For the several viewpoints of the major sciences concerning race, see UNESCO publication *The Race Question in Modern Science* (1956).

[13] See "The Effects of Segregation and the Consequences of Desegregation: A Social Science Statement," *Minnesota Law Review*, May, 1953, pp. 427-439, for the text of the statement and p. 427 for a list of the social scientists who drafted and signed the statement.

[14] *Op. cit.*, p. 109.

sideration by the Court of the effects of segregation on the children of the minority group. The Court said, "To separate them [Negro children] from others of similar age and qualifications solely because of their race generates a feeling of inferiority as to their status in the community that may affect their hearts and minds in a way unlikely ever to be undone."

The following statement by the Kansas court, which takes into account intangible psychological factors, was quoted in the Supreme Court's decision: "Segregation with the sanction of the law has a tendency to retard the educational and mental development of Negro children." Chief Justice Warren, speaking for the Court, then said: "Whatever may have been the extent of psychological knowledge at the time of Plessy v. Ferguson, this finding is amply supported by modern authority. Any language in Plessy v. Ferguson contrary to this finding is rejected." At least it seems that the findings of modern social scientists were used in reaching the conclusion that segregation as such violated the "equal protection" clause of the Fourteenth Amendment. From the viewpoint of the Court the inequality of the intangible factors alone made segregated educational facilities inherently unequal and inferior and hence a violation of a basic constitutional right of all citizens.

Still another factor that contributed to the climate favorable to the Court's decision of 1954 was the message and work of the churches. Pronouncements, such as the one made by the Federal Council of the Churches of Christ in 1946 condemning segregation, contributed something to the creation of an atmosphere favorable for the Court's action. More significant, however, has been and is the message proclaimed by the churches. The impact of that message may be largely intangible and difficult to measure; nevertheless it has been and is a major factor in America in molding public opinion. It should be admitted, of course, that the church's message is always superior to its practice. This fact stems, to a considerable degree, from the divine-human nature of the church. Its central message is from the Lord. From him it has received its commission. But it is also a very human institution, with the limitations of the human and fleshly, unable to escape entirely its environment.

This means that the message of the church not only creates tension between the church and its message on the one hand and the world and its practice on the other, but that its message also creates a very definite tension within the church itself. It is a tension that results from its sense of divine mission coupled with its consciousness of its human limitations. In no area is this sense of tension more acute in the contemporary period than in the field of race. Such tension within the Christian fellowship and between the church, at least its message, and the world is necessary if any progress is to be made toward the Christian ideal for the world.

CHAPTER TWO

Reactions to the Decision

The Supreme Court decision of May 17, 1954, created for the South her newest and in many ways her most perplexing dilemma. She wants to be law abiding. She does not want to isolate herself from the rest of the nation. Neither does she want to be a problem area for the nation as it faces the challenge of communism. On the other hand, the majority of her citizens, at least in the Deep South, did not and do not like the Court's decision. To desegregate her schools means a change in her cultural pattern, a pattern that has become thoroughly established and is considered almost sacred. Here was and is the South's dilemma—shall she obey the order of the Court and give up her "sacred" pattern of life, or shall she defy the Court and maintain her established ways. It is a very painful decision.

The reactions in the South to the Supreme Court's decision, as in the nation as a whole, have been many and varied. All we can do in this chapter is to suggest, in rather broad outline, some of the major types of reactions.[1]

Immediate Reactions

Most, although not all, of the reactions immediately following the Court's decision were favorable. In the main, the promptest and

[1] For rather thorough reports on the reactions in the South see Shoemaker's *With All Deliberate Speed* and *Neither Black Nor White* by Wilma Dykeman and James Stokely, a husband and wife writing team. The latter book was published by Rinehart (1957).

20

most favorable of these reactions were by religious groups. The National Council of the Churches of Christ released a statement only two days after the historic Court action, which included the following:

The unanimous decision of the Supreme Court that segregation in the schools is unconstitutional gives a clear status in law to a fundamental Christian and American principle. The decision will have far-reaching effects in the whole nation and the world.

It offers the promise of further steps for translating into reality Christian and democratic ideals. The decision is a milestone in the achievement of human rights, another evidence of the endeavor to respect the dignity and worth of all men.

... we know that the churches and individual Christians will continue to exert their influence and leadership to help the authorized agencies in the several communities to bring about a complete compliance with the decision of the Supreme Court. . . .

The decision was also promptly approved by the Synagogue Council of America and by the Catholic Interracial Council. Two distinctly Southern religious groups that approved the decision were the Presbyterian Church of the United States and the Southern Baptist Convention. The General Assembly of the former in its meeting of 1954 adopted the following statement:

Having in mind the recent decision by the Supreme Court of the United States concerning segregation, the Assembly commends the principle of the decision and urges all members of our churches to consider thoughtfully and prayerfully the complete solution of the problems involved. It also urges all of our people to lend their assistance to those charged with the duty of implementing the decision, and to remember that appeals to racial prejudice will not help but hinder the accomplishment of this aim.

The Southern Baptist Convention, the largest religious body in the South, adopted by an overwhelming majority the following recommendations of its Christian Life Commission in its convention, meeting in June, 1954:

In the light of the recent decision handed down by the Supreme Court of our nation . . . we recommend:

1. That we recognize the fact that this Supreme Court decision is in harmony with the constitutional guarantee of equal freedom to all citizens, and with the Christian principles of equal justice and love for all men.

2. That we commend the Supreme Court for deferring the application of the principle both as to time and procedure until the nation shall have had time to work out methods by which transition from the present practice may be effected.

3. That we urge our people and all Christians to conduct themselves in this period of adjustment in the spirit of Christ; that we pray that God may guide us in our thinking and our attitudes to the end that we may help and not hinder the progress of justice and brotherly love; that we may exercise patience and good will in discussions that must take place, and give a good testimony to the meaning of Christian faith and discipleship.

4. That we urge Christian statesmen and leaders in our churches to use their leadership in positive thought and planning to the end that this crisis in our national history shall not be made the occasion for new and bitter prejudices, but a movement toward a united nation embodying and proclaiming a democracy that will commend freedom to all people.

The Southern Baptist Convention had provided the background, to some degree, for this action of 1954 by a statement adopted by the convention in 1947 at St. Louis, which has been generally entitled "Race Relations: A Charter of Principles."[2]

Religious groups were not the only ones that endorsed the decision. Some politicians promptly approved or promised compliance with the Court's action. For example, a number of Southern governors, or at least governors of states "with a Southern exposure," pledged the cooperation of their states. Examples were Francis A. Cherry of Arkansas: "Arkansas will obey the law"; Theodore R. McKeldin of Maryland: "Our citizens and our officials will accept readily the United States Supreme Court's interpretation of our fundamental law"; Johnston Murray of Oklahoma: "Oklahoma has

[2] Free copies may be secured from the Christian Life Commission, 161 Eighth Avenue, North, Nashville 3, Tenn.

always followed the law, whatever it is"; Lawrence Wetherby of Kentucky, who said his state would "comply with the law"; and Frank Clement of Tennessee, who pointed out that the Supreme Court was supreme "in interpreting the law of the land." Even Governor Thomas Stanley of Virginia, who drastically changed his mind in six weeks, announced that he would call a meeting of local and state officials to "work toward a plan which shall be acceptable to our citizens and in keeping with the edict of the Court."

There were some school boards that voted to comply at once with the Court's decision. The Board of Education in Washington, D.C., ordered "complete desegregation" with the least possible delay.[3] Baltimore likewise promptly complied (June 3, 1954), in spite of the fact that 41.3 per cent of its population was Negro. There were scattering communities farther South that desegregated their schools soon after the Court's decision. One such community was Fayetteville, Arkansas, located in the Ozarks and the home of the University of Arkansas. The school board voted on May 22, 1954, to admit the few Negro high school students, eight to twelve, to the white high school rather than to provide transportation, board and room for them at Fort Smith or Hot Springs, as in the past. The school superintendent said, "Segregation was a luxury we no longer could afford."

Some state educational officials expressed the opinion that their states would comply with the Court's decree. This was true in Texas and in Virginia. The state superintendent of public instruction in Virginia said: "There will be no defiance of the Supreme Court so far as I am concerned. We are trying to teach school children the law of the land and we will abide by it." Later developments changed the picture in Virginia and to a less degree in Texas.

What happened after the initial reactions, which were mainly favorable? The Court, in a sense, gave a year's reprieve, when it postponed until the next year any decision about the implementation or

---

[3] For what appears to be an objective story and appraisal of the Washington experience, see the seventy-page booklet by Carl F. Hansen, assistant superintendent in charge of senior high schools in the District of Columbia, entitled, *Miracle of Social Adjustment: Desegregation in the Washington, D.C. Schools* (Anti-Defamation League of B'nai B'rith, 1957).

enforcement of its decision. During this time it seems that those who were favorable to the decision waited to see what would happen in May of 1955. On the other hand, those who disapproved the decision got busy. The first of the White Citizens' Councils was organized in Mississippi in July of 1954. The politicians also began to move in, and the old-fashioned Southern demagogue came into his own again. Many people in the South, who originally felt that desegregation was inevitable and were willing to make an adjustment to it, gradually developed a defiant attitude. From a some-time-but-not-now attitude some of them moved to a never-never attitude.

This change of attitude might cause one to ask: What would have happened if the Supreme Court had ordered immediate compliance? Was the extra year a mistake in strategy? There is no way to be sure about the answers to these questions. We do know, of course, that the year was used to crystallize sentiment against compliance and to perfect strategies to be used in an attempt to evade or to nullify the Court's decision.

Resistance to the Decision

How can the strong resistance to the Court's decision be explained? One major reason for the resistance which is not mentioned very frequently and which is rather intangible is the threat the decision poses to the "seamless garment of apartness," which has become a phase of Southern life. John Bartlow Martin describes apartness as being like a vine that was rooted in slavery and never uprooted but merely twisted by the Civil War. It now entangles everyone and everything "in a suffocating net from which no one, white or black, knows how to extricate himself." He says that the purpose of segregation is the "inflexible apartness of the races."

This apartness, which has a background of three hundred years of a master-slave relation—a superior-inferior concept—represents a way of life. It is true that the majority of the white people of the South have benefited very little from that way of life. They really have little at stake in it. Nevertheless, they have tended to glorify the

"Old South" and to get some vicarious satisfaction from contemplating it.

Some Southerners may deny that apartness is a part of the Southern racial pattern. They can and do cite the cordial friendly relations between white and Negro people in many Southern communities. As commendable as these relations frequently are, they would have to admit, however, that the relationship is maintained, essentially, on a very real apartness or caste basis. The Negroes and whites get along well in many of those communities because the Negro knows and stays "in his place." He conforms to the behavior traditions established for him by the white man. Let him step out of his place, whatever that is, and one will see how suddenly the so-called good relations are disrupted.

As one would expect, organized resistance groups have thrived in the South, particularly in the Deep South, since the Supreme Court's decree. There has been considerable evidence, in some sections, of a revival of the Ku Klux Klan. There has arisen a number of other and new prosegregation groups, one source listing twenty such groups or movements. Some of these are composed largely of underprivileged white people, while others deliberately seek to enlist the support of professional and business leaders. The program and philosophy of the movements, and in some cases of the individual units in those movements, vary from a single-minded concern with the segregation issue to opposition to Jews, Catholics, United Nations, income tax, and almost anything else that anyone might be against.

By far the most significant of the resistance groups are the White Citizens' Councils, which more recently have tended to drop the word "White" from their name. The first council was formed in Mississippi in July, 1954. The Court's delay of a year in implementing its decision gave the councils a good chance to get started. By the end of 1954 there were, so it is claimed, 110 councils in Mississippi, with 25,000 members. The first council outside Mississippi was formed in Selma, Alabama, in October, 1954, which has continued to be one of the strongest centers of resistance anywhere in the South. It has been estimated that there are at the present time about 550 to

600 councils, with approximately 250,000 members. Other resistance groups may number as many as 50,000 members.

To the councils, along with the political leaders who have capitalized on the controversy and the newspapers that agitate the problem, belongs the credit or the responsibility "for rallying a fourth of a nation against the law of the land." One reason for the strength and influence of the Citizens' Councils is the quality of leadership they have been able to enlist in some places. In the main, it is a middle-class movement, the leaders coming from the ranks of respected business and professional men, many of them prominent churchmen. The councils have "a terrible yearning for respectability." They have denied any intent to use violence, proposing to restrict themselves to legal processes. In the main, they have scrupulously avoided any entanglements with the Ku Klux Klan, although they have been labeled by some as "the uptown" or "the manicured" Ku Klux Klan.

All of the leadership of the councils is not as respectable as the preceding might imply. There are extremists who have captured the leadership of some council groups. It remains to be seen whether or not the more respected leaders and the more conservative elements in the movement can hold in proper check hotheaded rabble rousers who tend to be attracted to such movements. The Klan was originally a fairly respectable organization led by responsible citizens; it turned into "a lawless band of ruffians." Will the councils go the same route? Whether they do or not, they tend to create an atmosphere favorable to the use of force or violence.

Some Southerners who are favorable to the aims of the Citizens' Councils disagree with them concerning some of their methods and regret some of the effects of the movement. One regrettable effect, which stems to a considerable degree from the propaganda and spirit created by the councils, is the shutting off of discussion and debate. There are serious restrictions regarding freedom of speech in the South concerning the race issue. This has been true in both secular and religious circles. This is one of the most consequential casualties of the present controversy. How can there be a wise resolvement of any problem if people are not free to discuss it? It is increasingly difficult in the South for one even to maintain an objective attitude toward and approach to the Supreme Court decision and the problems it has created. Those who have sought to maintain a moderate position have found themselves labeled as extremists and radicals. Their position has become more precarious and untenable. C. A. McKnight, editor of the *Charlotte Observer*, recently said: "The Southern moderate . . . is finding out that the middle ground upon which he has been accustomed to stand is fast shrinking beneath him. Strong pressure from the extremes is forcing him to shut up, or to join the resistance movement."

The moderates who "shut up" become a part of the "silent assent" and melt into "faceless anonymity." From the viewpoint of many segregationists, one is either wholeheartedly for them, including their strategy, or he is definitely against them. There can be no middle ground. The price of dissent in the South can be terrifically high, particularly in rural areas and small towns. The price can be high not only for the Negro but also for the white man.

According to some extreme segregationists, the greatest enemy to their cause is what they label "the Southern renegade" who favors desegregation, or as they prefer to call it "integration," which is a word more charged with emotion than "desegregation." Others in their hierarchy of demons are the National Association for the Advancement of Colored People, the Northern press, and the Supreme Court itself. The latter was and is composed of nine old men, "high priests" of Washington, who had been "socialized and psychologized" and who followed the communist line in an attempt to establish a "black empire" in the South. The day of their decision was and is "Black Monday," a term coined by Mississippi's Congressman John B. Williams in a 1954 speech to the House of Representatives and later adopted and popularized as the title of a widely distributed pamphlet by Circuit Judge Tom P. Brady, also of Mississippi.

The responsibility for the preceding cannot all be placed on the Citizens' Councils. Some politicians must share the credit or blame.

They have sought to capitalize on the unrest and dissatisfaction. They have frequently been the spokesmen for the resistance movement.

James F. Byrnes, of South Carolina, in an address significantly entitled "The South Respects the Written Constitution," charged that the Supreme Court in its decision altered the Constitution, and that if the Court could do that, then five men, a majority of the Court, could make the Court a constitution-maker rather than a constitution-defender. He called the 1954 decision "an experiment in sociology" and "a tragedy."

United States Senator James O. Eastland, of Mississippi, has said that the "country has entered an era of judicial tyranny" as a result of the Supreme Court's decision and that the Court "responded to a radical, pro-Communist political movement."

One of the most vocal critics of the Court's decision has been Governor Herman Talmadge, of Georgia, who is now a United States senator. He claims that the Court has usurped authority that belongs to Congress and the people, has reduced the Constitution to "a mere scrap of paper" and has thrown down the gauntlet to those who believe "that the Constitution means what it says." Senator Strom Thurmond, of South Carolina, also has charged that the Supreme Court usurped the power of Congress in its decision of May, 1954, and its decree of May, 1955; and that it invaded the "specifically reserved rights of the States."

Reactions of Negroes

It was a Negro scholar, Charles S. Johnson, the late president of Fisk University, who said, "Of all the voices raised in this crisis the one most ignored has been that of the Southern Negro." And he is the one who has more at stake in the contemporary controversy than anyone else. The fact that he has been largely ignored does not mean that he has not reacted, that he has not spoken. At least the Negro leadership of the United States has been quite alert to and relatively vocal regarding the significance of the Court's decision.

Most Negro leaders have considered the separate-but-equal doctrine "pernicious and obviously undemocratic," "a tragic farce," and "self-contradictory." The doctrine, from the Negro viewpoint, has been religiously followed as to "separate" but almost wholly flouted as to "equality." The decision of May, 1954, was for them "the great decision," "the second emancipation," "a memorable decision," which initiated the last stage in race relations in the United States. Thurgood Marshall, who is chief counsel for the National Association for the Advancement of Colored People, and who had a major part in winning the favorable decision of the Court, appraised the decision as follows: "This decision gives the lie to Communist propaganda. . . . For once, our country can hold its head up, and for that I am eternally grateful. I am grateful, not just as a Negro, but as an American."

Following the Court's decision there was a stiffening of opposition by Negroes in general to any discrimination. They adopted, in some places, a method earlier used successfully by Gandhi in India, but a strategy that was new to the American scene. This strategy of nonviolent resistance was used in the bus boycott at Montgomery, Alabama. Since then it has been used to a limited degree elsewhere.

Although the vast majority of Negroes approved the decision, their reactions, generally speaking, have been relatively mild. One possible reason for the lack of marked enthusiasm regarding the decision among Negroes in general is their uncertainty and uneasiness about the future. This uneasiness may stem in part from an unwillingness to accept the full responsibilities that first-class citizenship will place upon them. Some of their own leaders have pointedly suggested that when desegregation comes Negroes must measure up to higher standards than they have in the past. Formerly they could explain away or rationalize their failures by saying that they were Negroes and did not have a chance.

Another possible reason for the lack of enthusiasm on the part of some Negroes concerning the Court's decision is fear of the white man. Some of their experiences since the decision would justify that fear. In a number of places Negroes who have supported any move for desegregation have experienced economic boycott and pressure. The chairman of the White Citizens' Council in one Alabama county said that the purpose of the council was "to make it difficult, if not impossible, for any Negro who advocates desegregation to find and hold a job, get credit, or renew a mortgage." In a small Mississippi city fifty-three Negroes signed a desegregation petition. All but six withdrew their names when they were either fired or threatened with dismissal. Lists of the signers were posted in the stores of the community, and merchants refused to sell to them. These are examples of what has happened in some sections of the South.

This type of pressure and boycott, which is thoroughly un-American and un-Christian, may help to explain the fact that so much of the Negro leadership for desegregation has come from Negro ministers, and that so frequently their children are the ones who apply for admission to white schools. The Negro minister is harder to reach with any type of economic reprisal.

Some resistance to the desegregation of schools is evident in the Negro community. This resistance to some degree results from the fear of reprisals, as suggested previously; it also results from fear by Negro parents of discrimination and violence against their children in mixed schools. There is also hesitation by some Negroes who profit from segregation. This is true of Negro schoolteachers. For example, the *Journal of Negro Education* carried an article in the Winter, 1955, issue entitled "Apprehension of Negro Teachers Concerning Desegregation in South Carolina." The Winter, 1957, issue included a considerable section devoted to favorable and unfavorable reactions of Negro teachers to the Supreme Court decision. Schoolteaching has been one of the best occupational opportunities for the better educated Negro. Many of the 75,000 to 80,000 teachers might lose their positions in a thoroughly integrated public school system.

We should remember, however, that the vast majority of Negro leaders, including their teachers and preachers, are active in the protest movement. They seem to be giving expression to the largely inarticulate cry of the surging masses, masses who are fearful, in many sections, to speak out for themselves. There is evident, however, even among the masses of Negroes a growing sentiment for the enforcement of the Supreme Court's decision and hence for desegregation. The Gallup Poll reported in December, 1957, that 69 per cent of Southern Negroes wanted the decision enforced, compared to 53 per cent two years earlier. Only 13 per cent were opposed to its enforcement.

Reactions of the Churches

The reactions of the churches, particularly of general denominational bodies, immediately following the Supreme Court decision were mentioned earlier. Here we want to set out, in rather broad outline, the reactions in the months and now years following the decision.

Much of this reaction, it will be admitted, is in the form of general pronouncements or statements. It may be, as some people frequently charge, that such pronouncements or resolutions are relatively ineffective as a means of social change, and that they even have comparatively little influence on the local church. They frequently deal in beautiful generalities and "sweet moralizing." Many times they fail to come to grips with the real issues, and do not spell out any next steps that may be taken in applying the Christian ideal. Nevertheless, these pronouncements have considerable influence on the churches and on the public in general.

Whatever may be one's appraisal of pronouncements by general church bodies, the ecumenical Christian movement and the major denominations have continued to speak out against segregation. For example, the World Council of Churches in its second General Assembly, that met in Evanston, Illinois, shortly after the Supreme Court's decision on school segregation, declared in a provocative message on race relations that the church should proclaim God's will regarding race "both in words and deeds." It gave as its judgment that "the whole pattern of racial discrimination is seen as an unutterable offense against God" and should be endured no longer. It further declared that "it is the duty of the Church to protest against any law or arrangement that is unjust to any human being."

Similarly, the General Assembly of the National Council of the Churches of Christ has recently spoken out, as it had on several previous occasions, against segregation. At its meeting in St. Louis in December, 1957, it said: "Racial segregation is contradictory to the teaching of Jesus." It also said: "The General Assembly of the National Council of Churches reaffirms at this time its renunciation of the pattern of racial segregation both in the churches and in society as a violation of The Gospel of love and human brotherhood."

Major denominations, such as the Episcopal Church,[4] the Methodist Church,[5] and the Presbyterian Church, U.S.A.,[6] have spoken and taken action against segregation in general and within the church. Particularly significant, however, from the Southern perspective, are the actions taken by the Presbyterian Church of the U.S. and the Southern Baptist Convention. The latter is by far the strongest, at least in numbers, of the religious groups in the region. The Presbyterian Church of the U.S., while not so strong in numbers, retains its Southern identity and carries a great deal of weight in the area.

It seems that sentiment against segregation and for desegregation in the General Assembly of the Presbyterian Church of the U.S. has increased in recent years. For example, an attempt was made at the ninety-fifth General Assembly (1955) to rescind the action of the previous year which had stated that segregation was un-Christian.

---

[4] See booklet entitled *Bridge Building in Race Relations*, with the subtitle "What the Episcopal Church Has Said and Done." The booklet is produced by the National Council, 281 Fourth Ave., New York 10, N.Y., and sells for fifty cents.

[5] See particularly the little pamphlet *The Methodist Church and Race*, single copies of which may be secured free from the Board of Social and Economic Relations of the Methodist Church, 740 Rusk St., Chicago 11, Ill.

[6] See several issues of a monthly publication *Social Progress*, but particularly the special issue for January, 1955, entitled "Segregation on Sunday," and the regular issue for January, 1957, which includes stories of several Presbyterian churches that have desegregated, and the issue for September, 1957, on "Desegregation," with several excellent articles.

Instead of rescinding the former action, which had been passed by a vote of 236 to 169, the assembly reaffirmed the action by a vote of 293 to 109.

In the ninety-seventh General Assembly (1957), meeting in Birmingham, a clearly worded statement was approved that condemned discrimination in the schools and scourged the Ku Klux Klan and the White Citizens' Councils, saying that "it is unthinkable that a Christian should join himself to Klan or Council." The complete statement of about four thousand words was approved "with a scattering of negative votes."

The Christian Life Commission of the Southern Baptist Convention has continued, in spite of some rather belligerent opposition, to bring recommendations to the Southern Baptist Convention regarding race relations in general, including segregation and desegregation. The convention, although there has been at times a very vocal protest, has continued to give overwhelming approval to the commission's reports and recommendations.

At the Houston meeting of the Southern Baptist Convention in 1958, the Christian Life Commission included in its report a section entitled "A Call for Racial Reconciliation." The closing paragraph of this section of the report was as follows:

This period of human conflict is a time of challenge to every citizen. He is called upon to help and not to hinder the progress of justice for all peoples. He is called upon to stand in defense of those cherished human freedoms that are the heritage of every American citizen. He must challenge the threat to the public school system of this nation which is one of the greatest factors in American history for the maintenance of democracy and of our common culture. We commend those ministers and laymen and the great body of women and young people who have taken their stand on these issues to the end that we may become a united nation embodying a democracy that insures justice and freedom for all.

Back at the grass roots there is still plenty of opposition to the statements approved by general denominational bodies. Evidently some of the messengers or delegates who support those statements and resolutions in the general meetings feel that they cannot support them in their local churches and communities. This situation stems, to some degree, from the fact that the general bodies are composed, in the main, of ministers. On the race issue, as on many other moral and spiritual matters, there is a considerable gap between the thinking and convictions of typical ministers and laymen.

Some of the most courageous and significant recent statements regarding segregation and desegregation have been made by ministerial groups. Each of these statements has had its own unique background that gives to it added weight. Space will not permit a discussion of the immediate occasion or background for the pronouncements, although in one or two cases this will be self-evident. In every instance these statements or pronouncements gave expression to a stirring of conscience among Southern ministers. They had kept silent as long as they could. They felt that they must speak. They could not be satisfied to remain as part of "the silent assent." They realized, as Liston Pope once said, that to do nothing was to align themselves in effect with the stronger or with the side that would profit most from their inertia. Some of them sensed, as Pope has said, that attempts at neutrality are immoral, and that "the effort to be all things to all men may eventuate in being little to anybody." This stirring of conscience took place at Little Rock and elsewhere. People are beginning to understand again that the prophet of God can be pushed only so far; when crowded too much he will proclaim courageously a "Thus sayeth the Lord."

Before "Little Rock" (January 28, 1957), the Richmond Ministers' Association released "A Statement of Conviction on Race," which was rather pointedly addressed to the governor and to the legislature of the state. It appealed for freedom of discussion but also for obedience to constituted authority. Regarding the latter, the ministers said:

To defy openly the Supreme Court and to encourage others to do so, in our judgment, is not only poor strategy; it is poor citizenship. Therefore, we urge our state government to act with loyalty and with maturity as regards co-operation with all established agencies of American government, and to lead us in a statesmanlike rather than an anarchistic manner.

The Richmond group also asked that local communities be permitted the privilege of deciding for themselves concerning the desegregation issue rather than for it to be handled on the state level.

In an evident reference to happenings at Little Rock, a statement released (October 15, 1957) by a large group of representative Houston ministers of all major religious faiths said the following: "Unfortunate and tragic events which have transpired elsewhere recently must not happen here!" While admitting that the courts are not infallible, the ministers said: "We do firmly believe that our courts are one of the bulwarks of our society." They further said that every God-fearing citizen should encourage respect for the courts. It was also their conviction that for an individual or a group to defy or encourage others to defy a decision simply because they did not approve it would "lead to anarchy in which the rights of none are respected."

A short time later (November 3, 1957), eighty Atlanta Protestant ministers also released a statement concerning the general racial situation. They admitted their own involvement in the problem, and frankly confessed that it had not been solved within the churches they served. They also said: "We are conscious that our own example in the matter of brotherhood and neighborliness has been all too imperfect. We do not pretend to know all the answers." They did say, however, that Christian people have a special responsibility for the solution of the racial problem, and expressed the conviction that if Christians would sincerely seek to understand and apply the teachings of Christ they would find the answer for the problem.

The Atlanta ministers also deplored the work of extremists on both sides, and the insistence by many people that integration meant amalgamation. They affirmed their conviction that the integrity of both races should be maintained "through the free choice of both." They further suggested that "all Americans, whether black or white, have a right to the full privileges of American citizenship."

They closed their statement with an emphasis on six principles, which the *Atlanta Constitution* called a "code for Christian conduct." The principles as summed up by the *Constitution* were as follows:

(1) Freedom of speech, without reprisal.
(2) An obligation to obey the law, as well as a right to try to change laws by legal means, but never by violence and economic reprisal.
(3) Preservation of the pubic schools.
(4) A condemnation of hate and scorn as never justified.
(5) Maintenance of communication between responsible leaders and the races.
(6) Consistent prayer for God's guidance.

Still later (April, 1958), approximately three hundred white Protestant ministers representing thirteen denominations in metropolitan Dallas signed a statement admitting their own prejudice and the failure of their "religious bodies to solve problems of racial relationships." They declared their conviction, however, that "racial problems and their solution are moral and spiritual as well as political matters." They plainly stated that "enforced segregation is morally and spiritually wrong." Obedience to the order of the courts was encouraged. The statement said, "If individuals or groups defy court decisions, they are inviting anarchy in which no one's rights will be preserved." The only solution for the whole racial problem was said to be "the application of the New Testament concept of Christian love in which we seek for others that which we desire for ourselves."

The statement by Dallas white Protestant ministers was followed by one from Negro ministers, similar in its over-all emphasis. There was still another declaration later formulated by a White Citizens' Council leader and signed by a large group of white ministers defending the segregation pattern.

This last fact suggests that the white ministers of the South do not all speak the same language regarding segregation. They roughly can be divided into three major groups, with all shades of opinion within each of those groups. There are those who defend segregation not only as a way of life but as in harmony with the will of God. They pronounce their blessings upon it. Then there are a great host of ministers, possibly a majority in most sections of the South, who believe segregation is contrary to the purposes of God but who have decided, at least for the present, to remain silent. They may follow this strategy out of fear, or out of a sincere conviction that in the long run it will serve best the kingdom of God among men. The third group, which in most sections, at least of the Deep South, is a small minority, not only believe that segregation is contrary to the will of God but also say so in private and from their pulpits.

"The New Reconstruction"

What will be the ultimate results in the South—will desegregation come gradually or never? To use an expression of C. Vann Woodward, will the "New Reconstruction" go the way of the Old Reconstruction? Legislative acts and Supreme Court decisions in the past have been largely nullified by public apathy or resistance. Will the New Reconstruction repeat the futility, frustration, and failure of the Old? No one can say for sure what the final outcome will be.

The old tragic pattern has tended to repeat itself. In the contemporary period, as in the 1860's, the South finds itself standing in defiance of the public policy of the nation. Now, as then, the border states have fallen away to go with the Union. "The roll call of the states that voluntarily abandoned segregation in the wake of the 1954 Supreme Court decision has a historic ring."[7] The states of the Upper South again, after some hesitation and with considerable division, have cast their lot with the states of the Deep South.

There are some differences, however, in the contemporary situation and the Old Reconstruction that may suggest the possibility of a more favorable ultimate outcome. In both Reconstructions the opposition has sought to unite the various elements of the opposition by appealing to racial prejudice and to the idea of white superiority. This time the appeal is not so successful as formerly. There is available too much scientific knowledge and we hope too much of the Christian spirit for the appeal to be as effective as formerly. There is also today "a cleavage between generations," which is a significant factor in the contemporary situation. World War II had a consider-

[7] Harry S. Ashmore, *An Epitaph for Dixie* (New York, Norton, 1957, 1958), p. 21.

able effect on many of the younger generation, making them much more tolerant of those of other races.

Today there is a "southland of many Souths." There is no longer a solid South. A Civil War, in a sense, is being fought within the soul of the South. It may be another "thirty-year war," but the immediate battle may not be as one-sided as it appears to be. It is basically not so much a battle between different segments of the South as it is a battle within the soul of the individual Southerner. The inner nature of the war or battle gives some hope for a more constructive outcome for the New than for the Old Reconstruction. Man will fight with himself only so long before he will sue for peace and come to terms.

The popular vote on some "segregation laws" or measures in certain states of the Deep South has revealed, in a sense, the division within the South. The approval of the measures was assured, but the strength of the opposition vote, usually overlooked, was surprising. Two or three examples will suffice: Georgia in November, 1954, by a vote of 210,488 to 181,148 approved a constitutional amendment permitting operation of a "private school" system; Mississippi in December of 1954 by a vote of 106,832 to 46,095 voted to give the legislature authority to close the public schools rather than submit to their desegregation; Virginia in January of 1956 by a vote of 304,154 to 146,164 approved the calling of a constitutional convention to permit the use of public funds for pupils attending private schools.[8] Notice the strength of the opposition vote in each case.

Another element of hope for the New Reconstruction is the increasing number of Negroes who are voting. The Negro vote in some of the population centers of the North and East has become a factor of real significance. It carries considerable weight with the national leaders of both parties.

The vote of the Southern Negro, which is constantly increasing, has also become an important factor on the political scene. It has been estimated that only 250,000 Negroes of the South voted in the 1940 elections but that 1,200,000 were registered in 1952 and possibly as many as 3,000,000 voted in 1956. Commenting on these figures,

[8] Shoemaker, *op. cit.*, pp. 98–99.

Liston Pope says that Negro voters have now reached a position in several states where they could represent the balance of power in elections.[9] There is no place where this is more true than in the states of the Deep South with their comparatively large Negro population. This fact has major significance for the present segregation-desegregation controversy. It represents a marked contrast between the New and Old Reconstructions. It at least creates enough of a potential problem to make many Southern politicians a little uneasy.

It is also true that in the New Reconstruction the minority group has a better trained leadership than during the former Reconstruction. No longer are the white people dealing with recently freed slaves. They are facing a people who are constantly improving their educational, economic, and political status. They will not accept as a final settlement of the present struggle anything that does not assure them full equality. Many of their leaders are capable men with a deep determination and a sense of divine purpose concerning the present struggle. Such leaders are not easily discouraged or defeated.

A major element of hope for the ultimate resolvement of the segregation problem is the conscience of the South. As much as any section of the nation, the South has prided herself on her loyalty to democratic principles and to the Christian way of life. Many of the people of the South recognize that there is no sound basis for democracy without respect for law and for those who interpret and enforce the law. There must be obedience to law or there is anarchy. The tradition that a man is a man "for all that" is also strong in the South, and it has been suggested that it is a strain to have to insert "white" before man. The "Bible belt" is likewise in the South.

Benjamin Muse, a former Virginia legislator, has said that there are many uneasy consciences and unhappy people in the South today. He concludes by saying: "Educated men who speak lightly of abolishing public schools, patriotic Americans who voice contempt of the government of the United States, Christians who flout the teachings

9 *The Kingdom Beyond Caste* (New York, Friendship Press, 1957), p. 67:

of the churches—these do not sleep well at night."[10] This uneasy conscience of the South, which helps to explain the vitriolic protest against the Court's decision, is one of the main hopes for a more favorable outcome of the New Reconstruction than of the Old.

Still another factor that may contribute to a more favorable ultimate outcome of the New Reconstruction is the revolution that is taking place in the South. The South is shifting from a rural to an urban economy. It is being rapidly industrialized. Farms are being mechanized at an unprecedented pace. All of these things, which are simply different phases of the revolution, are creating a climate more favorable to desegregation. They and other forces are "reshaping the Southern region in the nation's image."[11]

There is a revolution in progress not only in the South but also in the world. That revolution is pushing the entire world toward the equal treatment of all men. In such a period desegregation may be delayed for a period of time, but its eventual achievement is almost beyond question. Great world movements can be directed, to some degree, but they cannot be indefinitely postponed or defeated. The so-called New Reconstruction in the South is evidently a part of a broad and deep world revolution. In such a time, to adapt an expression of Liston Pope's, "change is not only possible; it is inevitable."[12]

It does seem that the pressure will be so great on the South, both from within and without, that sooner or later she will adjust and conform to the Supreme Court decree. In many sections when this is legally done it will actually make little difference in the generally accepted pattern of life.

[10] "When and How the South Will Integrate," *Harper's Magazine*, April, 1957, p. 53.
[11] Ashmore, *op. cit.*, p. 22.
[12] *Op. cit.*, p. 59.

CHAPTER THREE

Separation and Segregation

It would help in the contemporary racial discussion if clearer distinctions were made between certain words and if there was a more discriminating use of those words. There is also needed a better understanding of the relation of some of those words to one another.

Separation Versus Segregation

Some confusion has resulted from the failure of many people to distinguish between separation and segregation. Based strictly on the etymology of the words, they might be practically equated. It would make for clarity, however, if a distinction was made between a more or less voluntary separation of races and compulsory segregation, compulsory by custom or law or both.

There are cultural, national, and racial groups that tend voluntarily to isolate or to separate themselves from those of the majority or controlling group. The controlling group, incidentally, is not always a majority. Such is not the case in South Africa or in the Black Belt counties of the Southern states in America. Throughout this discussion, however, we shall consider the Negroes a minority group. Although they are not a minority in some localities, they are a minority from the American viewpoint, and are now an actual minority in every state of the Union.

The Negroes along with other isolated or separated groups form the national communities, the Chinatowns, the little Harlems that are found in many of the larger population centers of the American North as well as in the South. In other words, considerable separation takes place even in a legally desegregated society. In appraising the entire contemporary racial situation it will be well to remember that some Northern metropolitan centers, such as Philadelphia, maintained segregated schools as late as 1900.

There may be, and are, many factors contributing to a certain amount of separation, which is more or less natural and voluntary. There seems to be a natural desire by those who speak the same language, who have the same cultural background, or who are of the same color to group together for social fellowship.

This type of separation is generally more complete, more permanent, and more pathetic or unfortunate for the Negroes than for any other group. The second and third generations of most national and cultural groups are absorbed into the main stream of American life. They are at least classified as "white" in contrast to "colored." On the other hand, the Negro is something different, set apart; he is not counted in. He, who in one sense is more American than any of the others, is treated as less of an American than they. He belongs, yet he does not belong. This is one of his frustrating dilemmas.

Even those people who continue a more or less separated life, such as the Jews and the Orientals, are not so thoroughly isolated as the Negro. They are accepted at least within limits as partners in the American way. They have more contacts with the majority group on the basis of equality than the Negro. For the Jew, as an example, the separation may be, as one of their own number has said, a "separation at sundown." In other words, rather normal business contacts are maintained during the day, but there is little if any social fellowship within the family circle at the end of the day. For the Negro the separation is also from sunrise to sundown; it continues from birth to death.

Another thing that makes the American Negro's separation particularly difficult for him is the fact that he does not have a national or a well defined cultural background to sustain him. He has been in America so long that he has become a part of America. There may remain some African overtones, but even those overtones have become Americanized. They have been woven into the fabric of the American way, and have become, along with the contributions of other national, cultural, and racial groups, an integral and an important phase of the American way of life.

Why is there a tendency for Negroes, as well as those of other minority groups, to separate themselves more or less voluntarily from the majority or dominant group? Notice the use of the words "more or less." That which seems on the surface to be voluntary may not be when examined more carefully. In addition to the desire to be with their own people, the tendency to withdraw may also be a defense mechanism. They may believe that they are not wanted among the majority group. People do not feel at ease where they are not wanted. They may feel embarrassed, insecure, or even inferior in the presence of the majority.

When those of the minority group are with their own people they have more of a sense of being wanted, respected and loved. They find in such association a greater degree of security and significance. These are among the basic needs of the human person. All of this means that the more unfriendly the majority group, the stronger will be the trend on the part of the minority to withdraw or to separate from the main stream of social life and contact. This, in turn, means that separation which may be, to a degree, natural and voluntary, may, on the other hand, stem to some extent from social ostracism and pressure by the controlling group. Separation caused by the latter might be voluntary, but it would not necessarily express a natural desire or inclination. It would be the choice of the lesser of two evils. Such separation would approach, if it could not be identified with, segregation. If such an identification is made, the word "voluntary" should precede and define segregation. A South African writer makes a distinction between what he calls "passive" segregation, based on culture and tradition, and "active" segregation, that is enforced by law. [1] Such "passive" or "voluntary" segregation could properly be equated

[1] Ben J. Marais, *Colour: Unsolved Problem of the West* (Cape Town, South Africa, Howard B. Timmins, n.d.), p. 82.

with separation only when the initiative for the separation was taken by the Negro or by the minority group. It becomes segregation in the purer sense of the word when the predominant factor in the separation is the attitude or demands of the controlling group. Liston Pope defines segregation as follows: "Segregation means the enforced separation of racial groups, either in regard to a few areas of life or in regard to many or all." [2] The key word in this definition is "enforced." This force may be by custom rather than by law.

The most thorough segregation is where it is maintained by law. This is "legal" segregation which is "compulsory." Many times those laws, as is true to a considerable degree of laws in general, are merely the crystallization and formalization of generally accepted customs. In turn, in a segregated society, its customs and taboos are justified and defended at times by an appeal to the segregation laws. The National Council of the Churches of Christ, in a statement adopted in 1952, defined segregation as "the externally imposed separation or division of individual persons or groups, based on race, color or national origin." The statement further said: "In many places segregation is established and supported by law. In others it is almost as rigidly enforced by social customs and economic practices."

Separation and Segregation

Not only would a clearer understanding of the distinction between separation and segregation be helpful in the present discussions concerning race, but it would also be helpful if people generally understood the relatedness and the influence of these two on each other. For example, in a segregated society there may be marked or comparatively little separation of the races. It is possible even within the pattern of segregation to have rather free and frequent intermingling of those of the majority and the minority groups. This has been true in many communities in the Deep South. The extent of the intermingling has been and will be determined, to a considerable degree, by the acceptance of or the adjustment to a more or less permanently

[2] *The Kingdom Beyond Caste*, p. 80.

secondary status by the minority group. As long as those of the minority group "stay in their place," they may have considerable freedom of movement and also considerable security.

This may help to explain the fact that there has been less communication since the Supreme Court decision of May, 1954, between Negroes and white people in many areas than was formerly true. It is possible that the separation of the races in some sections of the South is more complete now than at any time in the past. This modern tendency toward social isolation began before the Court's decision. As more Negroes became better educated, they tended to isolate themselves from the white community. They no longer fitted into the Negro-white mold of the South. However, the same thing took place in the North, where the white people tended, more than in the South, to grant the Negro his basic citizenship rights. This was accompanied, however, at least in many sections of the North, by increasing isolation.

This isolation, North and South, was both voluntary and compulsory. In other words, much of it stemmed from the attitude of Negroes as well as white people. One factor in this separation that many white people do not but should understand is the rise of a new type of Negro—at least one who is rather drastically different from his forefathers. In increasing numbers this "new" Negro is refusing, even in sections of the Deep South, to accept a secondary status without protest. He is more militant and more vocal than in the past. These facts have tended to force the Negro into increasing isolation. This is one reason why the struggle for desegregation may more or less inevitably lead, for at least a time, to more pronounced separation of the races.

The more formal and the more firmly established the segregation pattern, the greater the resistance to its change by the segregating group. In turn, the greater the resistance to change the greater the trend toward the isolation, both voluntarily and by compulsion, of those who would seek to change that pattern. Such isolation may be the experience even of those of the majority group who approve or are suspected of approving any change in the customary pattern of race relations.

In a segregated society, a thoroughgoing caste structure tends to develop with fixed customs, mores, and taboos governing almost every aspect of the relations of the majority and minority groups. [3] The "good" member of the minority group from the perspective of the majority group is one who conforms consistently to the generally accepted pattern—a pattern determined and maintained by the majority or segregating group.

Rather strangely and somewhat inconsistently, some people who will not defend segregation on the basis of principle justify its existence "by reference to history and established pattern." They defend segregation on the basis of the more or less natural tendency for those of one race to separate from those of other races. They argue, for example, that since Negroes prefer to be together, as is evidenced to some degree by residential separation in cities of the North where there is no legal segregation, segregation laws are justified.

The defenders of the segregation pattern, who use the preceding argument, evidently fail to see one inconsistency in their reasoning. Really, if Negroes naturally prefer to be by themselves, why should anyone fear or oppose desegregation? If they would voluntarily maintain separation, what would any community or state lose if it repealed its segregation laws? Voluntary separation would be a more logical argument for desegregation than for segregation.

The segregation pattern in the Southern region of the United States developed over a considerable period of time. Before the emancipation of the Negroes, few of them received any formal education; hence, there was neither segregation nor integration in the schools. Many of the Negroes, however, belonged to the same churches as white people, the First Baptist Church of Montgomery, Alabama, reporting six hundred Negro and three hundred white members at the end of the war between the states. In some churches

[3] A book written some years ago, but which is still largely relevant, is Bertram Wilbur Doyle's *The Etiquette of Race Relations in the South* (Chicago, University of Chicago Press, 1937).

the Negroes sat with the white people, while in others they were provided for in a special section of the church building, which was frequently the balcony.

Segregated public schools were provided during the Reconstruction period. Negroes took the initiative about the same time in a large-scale separation or withdrawal from the white churches. One reason for their separation was their inferior status within those churches. After the separation of Negroes and whites there was relative peace and harmony between them for many years. The Negroes had considerable freedom of movement within most areas. Gradually, however, there were increasing restrictions and hence growing tension between the races.

In the midst of this mounting tension, and partly as a result of it, Booker T. Washington delivered his famous "Compromise Address" in Atlanta in 1895. The address included the frequently quoted statement: "In all things that are purely social we can be as separate as the fingers, yet one as a hand in all things essential to mutual progress." The next year (1896) the Supreme Court of the United States gave its approval to the separate-but-equal doctrine in the Plessy v. Ferguson case. There followed an extensive web of legislation—community as well as state—that defined and enforced segregation. It was rapidly extended to increasing areas of life until by 1910 it was firmly established in most realms. Thus although Jim Crow practices had existed in some ways from the slave days, yet Jim Crowism as a formal system in the South is only about fifty or sixty years old. [4]

Why has the strict segregation pattern become so firmly established and so vigorously defended? One factor of major significance has been and is racial prejudice, which it seems can be as easily aroused, as quickly transformed into action, and as difficult to control as any type of prejudice. Prejudice, to use a popular expression, is being down on what one is not up on. It is a prejudgment, a judgment not based on knowledge or experience. It implies an opinion based on insufficient

[4] See C. Vann Woodward, *The Strange Career of Jim Crow* (New York, Oxford University Press, 1955).

or irrelevant data. It is attended with a tendency to generalize on too few specific instances. It encourages what has been called the "lumping fallacy." Its language in the area of race is, "All Negroes are . . ." For example, one member of the group commits a crime; all members of the group are stigmatized. Prejudice fails to think of individuals as individuals; they are classified as members of a particular group or race. [5]

The strength of one's prejudice seems to be closely related to his level of anxiety. If everything is moving along smoothly, with peace within and harmony without, prejudices lie largely dormant. But they "burst forth with renewed intensity when security is disturbed." [6] In the contemporary period prejudices have been released in many sections that had been relatively quiet for a long time. Many individuals have discovered in themselves a depth of racial prejudice that they did not dream was there. Even relatively mature Christians frequently express racial prejudice under certain conditions. Those conditions evidently are quite prevalent in the contemporary period.

Unfortunately, some people today are making the arousing of racial prejudice their business. An appeal to prejudice gives to them their greatest opportunity for recognition and leadership. They seek to arouse prejudice in others in order to make themselves popular. They are the political, religious, and social demagogues, who have been and are a curse to the South. Some of these men, particularly those whose popularity has depended entirely on the present racial situation, might be shrugged off if it was not for the memory of Adolf Hitler, who used some of the same strategies and techniques as the race baiters of the present day.

The strength of racial prejudice, along with the ease with which it

[5] For an excellent small book on racial prejudice, see Hortense Powdermaker, *Probing Our Prejudices* (New York, Harper, 1944). Arnold Rose has a concise pamphlet, entitled *The Roots of Prejudice*, published by UNESCO. A recent book is Kenneth B. Clark's *Prejudice and Your Child* (Boston, Beacon Press, 1955). For a thorough scholarly discussion see George Simpson and J. Milton Yinger, *Racial and Cultural Minorities* (New York, Harper, 1953).

[6] *Psychiatric Aspects of School Desegregation*, p. 17.

can be aroused, is one reason that the general racial outlook, at least as far as constructive action is concerned in several Southern states, has been reduced to the level of the most prejudiced minority. Extremely prejudiced minorities have prevented many communities in the South from complying with the decree of the Supreme Court. Some state legislatures have been dominated by the representatives of Black Belt counties. One reason for this is the fact that they have representation in the legislatures out of proportion to their population. "For example, in Alabama 16 Black Belt counties with 13.5 per cent of the state's total population have 27.3 per cent of the House representation and 28.5 per cent of the Senate seats."[7] There exists a similar situation in Georgia, Louisiana, and Mississippi.

It should be remembered that racial prejudice is both a cause and an effect of segregation. This is another one of those vicious circles which plague us in many areas. The more strongly prejudiced people are, the more firmly they defend and maintain the segregation pattern. In turn, segregation tends to perpetuate conditions that are used to justify segregation and to deepen and to solidify prejudice. This is true in a segregated society even when there is considerable intermingling of the races. A deep and significant psychological separation may exist even when there is not a great deal of physical separation. It seems impossible to maintain races in a superiority-inferiority status without real psychological isolation, which in turn is a major factor in a deep-seated prejudice which affects those of the minority as well as those of the majority group.

Racial prejudice is expressed in many different ways. One very prevalent mode of expression is the oft stated opinion that Negroes are innately inferior to white people. This is a prejudgment—a generalization for which there is little if any factual or scientific support. This idea of the natural inferiority or superiority of races which is classified as "racism" has been labeled "man's most dangerous myth."[8]

[7] Shoemaker, *With All Deliberate Speed*, p. 134.
[8] M. F. Ashley Montagu, *Man's Most Dangerous Myth* (3rd ed.; New York, Harper, 1952).

"A myth provides an apparently rational answer to an apparently insoluble problem. Such myths are maintained without regard to any demonstrable validity."[9]

Whether or not the idea of the innate inferiority and superiority of races is a myth, it has been used and is being used to support the segregation pattern. This concept was introduced into the United States as a well formulated theory by Madison Grant and Lothrop Stoddard. Their work in turn was based on the writing of the Frenchman De Gobineau and the British-born but German naturalized Houston Stewart Chamberlain. At least one contemporary scientist has said that "the question of 'racial superiority' . . . has never really been examined scientifically."[10]

In the contemporary controversy over school desegregation considerable emphasis has been given to the difference in the educational achievements of Negro and white children. This difference, which does pose a relatively serious problem, has been advanced by some people as an evidence of the inborn inferiority of the Negroes. It might just as properly be considered an evidence of a generally inferior social, economic, and cultural environment for the Negro child, including inferior educational opportunities and stimuli. It may be, as H. Bentley Glass, son of missionary parents, biologist at John Hopkins University, and a member of the school board of Baltimore which has desegregated its schools, has said, that differences in intelligence do exist, but that "differences in opportunity also exist, and until opportunity is equalized no one can say what is inherent by natural law." Really, the fact that the Negro child is retarded as compared with the white child might be used as an indictment against segregated schools. It might be evidence that segregated schools, as is true of segregation in general, mean discrimination, that segregated facilities are always inferior.

If it could be proved conclusively that Negroes generally were

[9] *Psychiatric Aspects of School Segregation*, p. 17.
[10] William C. Boyd, *Genetics and the Races of Man* (Boston, Little Brown, 1950), p. 185.

innately inferior, would this necessarily justify segregation? What about the considerable overlap between Negro and white pupils in ability? Some of the former are quite evidently superior rather than inferior in native ability and in educational achievement to some of the latter. If segregation is to be based on the idea of innate inferiority, then what is to be done with the superior individuals of the minority group? Also, what should be done with the white children who are inferior? If segregation is to be maintained, it seems that it will have to be on some basis other than the supposed inferiority and superiority of races.

It is possible that all the debate about the supposed inferiority and superiority of races is beside the point. Real equality does not depend upon achievement tests, educational progress, or upon scientific findings of any kind. The Negro's right to equal treatment before the law rests upon the single and simple fact that he is a man as other men. Men are not created equal in ability, but they are equally men, equal in all that basically makes them men, and are to be treated as equals before the law. This is the American ideal, which is soundly based on Christian principles.

Furthermore, from the Christian perspective it makes little difference if the Negro or any other racial group is superior or inferior. The Christian recognizes that God has created man, all men, in his own image. He recognizes that God is no respecter of persons and shows no partiality. He knows also that Christ died for all men, and that the salvation that is offered in Christ is available to all on the same basis. Those who through faith have come into the spiritual family of God are brothers and sisters in Christ. They all can and do pray that universal, unifying prayer "Our Father." Regardless of class or color, every child of God is a brother and should be "a brother beloved."

Furthermore, the Christian ethic demands that the strong serve the weak. There is not the least justification in the Christian message for the strong to lord it over the weak. The Negro, at least in our society, is in an inferior position. What if it could be proved conclusively—

which definitely has not been done—that he is innately and incurably inferior? What would this mean from the Christian viewpoint? It would simply mean increased responsibility for the supposedly superior group. A basic spiritual and scriptural principle is as follows: "To whom much is given, of him will much be required" (Luke 12:48). Any advantage any group has by nature or by circumstance increases that group's responsibility to society and to God.

Segregation and Discrimination

Segregation seems inevitably to involve some discrimination. This should be expected, since segregation is an extension, at least in the United States, of the master-slave tradition into a free society. It certainly involves discrimination when it is based on the idea that the segregated group is inferior, and when it is an expression of prejudice. And it is very doubtful if there would be any segregation, although there might be some voluntary separation, if there were no prejudice and no concept of superiority and inferiority. Segregation as such, with its element of compulsion, implies the inferiority of the segregated group. This in itself is discrimination. For example, the exclusion of Negro children, in a white-controlled society, from schools where white children attend denotes the inferiority of the Negro and not that of the white.

Historically, segregation and discrimination have been closely related. This has been true of the Jew in Europe, of the "untouchables" in India, as well as of the Negro in the United States. "History has never yet given evidence of a case where one group has segregated another group for other than selfish reasons. . . . The segregators only later came to the conclusion that segregation is in the interests of the segregated group."[11] The South African further says that the argument that segregation is "in the interests of the segregated group, is merely a narcotic for the conscience, adduced after the fact, to justify a selfish or a complacent policy."[12]

[11] Taken from *"Colour": Unsolved Problem of the West* by Ben J. Marais and published by Howard B. Timmins (Pty.) Ltd., Cape Town, South Africa.
[12] *Ibid.*, p. 238.

The fact that discrimination attends segregation has been quite evident in every area of our segregated society. Our separate-but-equal doctrine has been a failure, a myth. That failure has been particularly evident in the field of education. There were inequalities in the education of Negroes from the first. The more modern expressions of those inequalities stem, however, from the more vocal consciousness of the so-called "poor white" people in the 1890's. Their economic competition with Negroes became particularly acute. The latter were almost completely disfranchised, and their subordinate status was given a legal basis. This was the beginning of the Jim Crowism of the rawest sort. It was in this kind of atmosphere that the Plessy v. Ferguson decision, with its separate-but-equal doctrine, was made by the United States Supreme Court. It is significant that this development is less than seventy-five years old, not something with "hundreds of years" of standing, as defenders of the generally accepted social pattern have claimed in recent years.

In 1912, sixteen years after Plessy v. Ferguson and its separate-but-equal pronouncement, fifteen Southern states and the District of Columbia spent $10.32 for each white child for teachers' salaries and only $2.89 for each Negro child. Rather interestingly, the disparity between the per capita spent for white and Negro children increased with the increase in the percentage of Negroes in the population of the counties of the South. For example, in the counties where Negroes constituted less than 10 per cent of the population, the per capita spent for Negroes was $7.23 as compared to $7.96 for white children. In contrast, in counties where Negroes constituted 75 per cent or more of the population, the per capita expenditure for Negro children was only $1.78 as compared to $22.22 per white child.

While marked progress has been made in equalizing the expenditures for Negro and white children in recent years, there are some things that should be remembered about this progress. First, the Negro schools generally, although there have been and are some notable exceptions, have been and are so inferior to the white schools that equalization of expenditures would simply maintain the existing inequalities between Negro and white schools. To equalize facilities would mean that much more would have to be expended for Negro schools per child than for white schools. Incidentally, this has been done and is being done in some places.

A second thing that should be remembered about the movement to equalize facilities is its timing and its obvious motive or purpose in some places. There was increasing pressure on school authorities, from Negroes and from some white people, for better facilities for the Negroes. Some public officials were discerning enough to see the handwriting on the wall. They began to attempt to get their house in order. Some evidently hoped and some still hope to satisfy the Negro with better schools—schools of which they can be proud—and thus reduce if not eliminate the pressure for desegregation.

With all of the improvements that have been made, the general rule is that marked inequalities still exist. For example, approximately a year before the Supreme Court decision of May, 1954, a reporter for a leading Southern newspaper found a shocking difference in the expenditures for Negro and white children in many counties of Mississippi. Hinds County, where the state capital is located, spent $146 per white pupil and only $43 per Negro pupil. The reporter found, as others have before and since, that the proportion of the population that is Negro increases the disparity between the per capita expenditures for Negro and white children. Alcorn County, for example, with only 14 per cent of its population Negro, spent $82 per white child and $71 per Negro child. In contrast, Tunica County, with 81 per cent of its population Negro, spent $270 per white child and only $21 per Negro child. Calhoun County, with 23 per cent of its population Negro, spent $87 per white child and $49 per Negro child. In contrast, Claiborne County, with 74 per cent of its population Negro, spent $387 per white child and only $40 per Negro pupil.

The history of segregation, in schools and in general, is a history of inequality. Segregation is always discriminatory; it has meant and does mean inferior service to the segregated. To expect a majority not to discriminate at least to some degree against the minority segregated group is to expect too much of human nature, unless that nature has been thoroughly redeemed. In turn, if men were thoroughly redeemed, it is doubtful if they would maintain a segregated society.

What if the facilities in a segregated society could be literally and fully equalized? What if there was no overt discrimination? Would there still be some discrimination? In other words, is discrimination inherent in segregation? It is if we agree with Benjamin Mays, Negro educator and Christian statesman. He says that segregation punishes a person for being what God made him and for circumstances over which he has no control. Segregation inevitably means discrimination also if we consider the inner or psychological effects on the segregated. A well trained Negro educator quietly but with deep emotion said to a group of white students: "You do not really know what segregation means. I do. I am among the segregated." Those students, along with their teacher, will never get away from the impact of that statement. Benjamin Mays says that "segregation is the greatest curse that can be imposed on anyone."

It was Charles Sumner who said, in pleading the case of Sarah Roberts before the Massachusetts Supreme Court (1850): "A separate school though *well* endowed would not secure that precise equality which they [Negro children] would enjoy in the common schools. . . . Segregation from the mass of citizens is of itself an inequality. . . . It is a vestige of ancient intolerance against a despised people."

While segregation is particularly discriminatory against the segregated, yet the results may be unfortunate for those of the majority group who sympathize with the struggles of the segregated. Segregation may be a "two-edged sword." Some have discovered that "a breadwinner must watch his tongue on race matters in the South." White people may also suffer, though their suffering may be "only of the spirit."[13]

[13] June Purcell Guild, "Whites Suffer Too," the *Christian Century*, Nov. 20, 1957, pp. 1382–83.

The Cost of Segregation

Segregation accompanied by discrimination is costly. Even if segregation could be indefinitely maintained, there is some question whether or not it could be afforded. It is very expensive from the economic viewpoint, which is one of its smallest prices. As suggested previously, some states that maintain segregated schools have found it very expensive to attempt to equalize, even in a limited way, the Negro and white schools. The State of Louisiana, for example, in a decade increased its expenditures for public school instruction for Negroes 400 per cent, while the Negro school population increased less than 38 per cent. Even with this sharp increase the schools were not equalized. There are some communities, even in the Deep South, where the cost of education is practically doubled because they maintain a segregated system, although there are comparatively few Negroes of school age. In some cases Negro scholastics are so few that they are transported to or boarded in another school district.

The cost of the dual school system, however, is only a comparatively small part of the total economic cost of segregation in general. There is no way to compute with any degree of accuracy what segregation costs the United States each year. One estimate has put the figure as high as fifteen to thirty billion dollars a year for discrimination in general. Segregation has definitely been a factor in the economic problems of the South, the region where the segregation pattern is maintained most rigidly. It may be that the South is no longer the nation's Number One economic problem, as she was labeled a few years ago; and it may be that the South's problems have stemmed, to some degree, from the devastation of the war between the states and the Reconstruction period; however, her treatment of the Negro in her midst has been a serious economic handicap. It was Booker T. Washington who said that one cannot hold a man down in the ditch without staying down there with him. The white South cannot hold the Negro down without staying down with him. This means economically as well as every other way. Imagine, for example, the increased purchasing power of the Negro and what that could mean to the Southern economy if the Negro, through the years, had had better job opportunities and had been paid a better wage. There is no way of knowing what the contemporary racial situation in certain areas is costing those sections in business and industrial development.

We are not concerned primarily, however, with the economic cost of segregation. There are other costs that are much more significant from the regional, the national, and particularly from the Christian viewpoint. Martin Luther King has said that segregation "sears the soul of both the segregator and the segregated." We should be much more concerned about the effects of segregation on the souls or lives of the segregated and the segregating than we are about financial costs.

When the psychological effects of segregation are considered we are, to use the words of the group of social scientists who signed a statement that was used by the plaintiffs in the cases before the Supreme Court when it made its May, 1954, decision, "on the frontiers of scientific knowledge." This same group did cite, however, the fact-finding report on the effects of prejudice, segregation, and discrimination on the personality development of children that was prepared as a basis for discussion and deliberation by the Mid-Century White House Conference on Children and Youth. The report suggested that prejudice, segregation, and discrimination and their social concomitants potentially damage the personalities of all children—those of the majority segregating group as well as those of the minority segregated group.

Children of the segregated group may react by overt aggression and hostility, which may be directed toward those of their own group or toward those of the segregating group. They may tend, from the psychological viewpoint, to hate themselves, to reject their group, to develop hostility toward other groups and society in general, all of which may eventuate in a general pattern of personality disorganization and difficulty. Some of the segregated group may react to racial frustration and conflict by withdrawing and submitting. This occurs more frequently among the middle and upper classes. Children of the minority group tend in general to develop a defeatist attitude, with a lowering of personal ambition. This is accompanied by a lower pupil morale and "a depression of the educational aspirational level." This helps to explain the lower achievement level of Negro pupils as compared to white children of the same age and grade. Thus segregation, even if facilities could be equalized, would be detrimental to most if not all members of the segregated group. This is the opinion of 90 per cent of a group of social scientists who replied to a question concerning the probable effects of enforced segregation.

It is not so easy to measure the effects of segregation on those of the majority or segregating group. It does seem, however, that there are some bad effects on many children and adults. Some children of the segregating group develop hostile feelings, which are symptomatic of a disordered personality. Many of them also develop guilt feelings and a general sense of frustration. They have been taught democratic principles and some of them the Christian ethic. They find, in general, that the principles of democracy and the Christian ethic are not applied to the area of race relations. They may develop a sense of guilt because they themselves do not consistently apply the spirit and principles that are a part of their heritage to this area of their lives. Those who are more perceptive may see that the fault is not entirely theirs, that it must be shared by the society in which they live. Some of these, both children and adults, will be frustrated and tend to become cynical. This frustration, particularly for children and youth of both the majority and the minority groups, tends to be deepened drastically when they realize that the very imperfect application of the ideals of our way of life to the racial situation is supported by the very ones who profess to believe and to teach those ideals to the younger generation. These are matters that increasingly disturb the intelligent members of the majority group, adults as well as children. The sensitive soul can never fully escape this feeling of frustration and conflict.

Segregation and discrimination not only affect the minority and the majority groups as such; they also affect their relations one to another. The majority, at best, develops a paternalistic, or what someone has called a "mascot" attitude toward the segregated. Paternalism involves the condescending service of a superior to an inferior. It seldom allows the "child" it nurtures to grow into full manhood. The member of the minority group may be accepted as a mascot for the team, but never as a fully participating member of the team.

Even where there is prevalent the paternalistic-mascot attitude, the so-called "vicious circle theory" operates.[14] Majority prejudice and discrimination keep the standards of living, health, education, culture, and morale of the segregated group low. This, in turn, as suggested earlier, contributes to the continuance of prejudice by the majority group. Thus, majority prejudice and minority low standards mutually cause and support one another. The main hope for a change is that one of the two factors will change. If it does, then it seems that inevitably the other will change. For example, relaxing or reducing of prejudice and discrimination will tend toward an improvement of the standards of living and culture of the segregated group. In contrast, an increase in prejudice and discrimination will contribute to a lowering of the standards of the minority group.

The fact that there tends to be a balancing between prejudice on the one hand and the standards and level of living on the other does not mean necessarily that all is peaceful. There is never an exact balancing of the two, and hence there is, in a sense, an "eternal conflict" between the segregated and the segregating. There is a tendency for the pressure from beneath from the segregated to be cumulative. As discrimination by the segregating is relaxed, which is usually done only under pressure, there tends to be an increasing pressure from the segregated for full equality of opportunity and the elimination of all discrimination. At times the cumulative effect of this increasing pressure becomes irresistible, as has been proven true in the contemporary period in many sections of the world. It remains to be seen if it will be true of the Negro minority in the United States.

In counting the cost of segregation, it will be wise for us to remem-

---

[14] See Gunnar Myrdal, *An American Dilemma* (New York, Harper, 1944), I, 75ff.

ber that the world, including the restless masses, have the United States under the severest scrutiny. The race problem in America is not just a Southern problem or even just a national problem. It has become, in the contemporary period, an international problem of the first magnitude. The United States has been considered the world's greatest democracy—the land of the free and the home of the brave. Its pledge of allegiance, widely known by other peoples, says that we are "one nation, indivisible, with liberty and justice for all." The peoples of other sections of the world are asking if Americans really mean what they say or if their democratic claims are false. Those peoples want to know if we intend to apply consistently our democratic principles to the minority peoples in our midst, or if we intend merely to give lip service to democratic ideals. They ask if we salute one or two flags, if we have one pledge of allegiance or two. They ask if we really have a colony in our midst, with our own colonial peoples, while we claim we have no colonies and want none.

The challenge of communism makes the situation even more acute for America and for the West. Two great forces, democracy and communism, are competing for mastery in the world, mastery over the minds and souls of men. Unfortunately for us, communism, in the area of international politics, has frequently become the champion of the rights of the underprivileged, including colonial peoples, most of whom are colored. On the other hand, because of their deep involvement in the colonial system, some of the nations of Western Europe have often resisted the latter-day equivalents of their own earlier revolutions. These nations of Western Europe are the allies of the United States, and hence our nation seemingly has frequently been forced into the unpleasant and difficult position of defending colonialism and opposing peoples who were fighting a battle similar to the one we fought to win our independence. As a result our influence among the colonial peoples of the world and the masses in general has sharply declined. Our prestige has been further damaged, to a drastic degree, by our treatment of the colored peoples in our midst. The masses of the world tend to identify their struggle with the struggle of our colored citizens.

Even if segregation did not damage our foreign relations it would be and is damaging to us. It violates what has been termed the American Creed. This conflict between the American Creed and its very imperfect application to race relations disturbs the conscience of many sensitive American white men, North and South. This conflict creates the kind of tension that will move people to seek to bring principle and practice closer together, or will lead them in desperation to deny the validity or the relevance of the Creed or principle. The latter, however, is not an abidingly satisfying or successful way out of the dilemma. It merely drives the conflict deeper underneath the surface, which will mean more serious disturbances in the future. Really, the fundamental principles of our way of life have been too ingrained in our thinking, they have permeated our thought patterns too deeply to be summarily dismissed or brushed aside. We cannot indefinitely ignore them. They demand recognition and at least an honest effort toward application.

Thus it seems that America, to save her own soul as well as to retain or regain her leadership in the world, which the world desperately needs, must work out some solution for the race problem consistent with the American Creed. Furthermore, if our nation is to retain the sense of purpose, direction, and unity which is essential to the strength of a nation, we must in some way bring our largest minority group into that unity. As Myrdal so pungently has said, *"America is free to choose whether the Negro shall remain her liability or become her opportunity."*[15] It now seems, more than a decade after Myrdal wrote, that time is fast running out. The world awaits the decision of America.

We have not touched, except in a very indirect way, on the cost of segregation to the churches and to the Christian movement in general. This will be done in a more specific way in a later chapter. It should be said here, however, that the race issue is American Christianity's test case. The future of organized Christianity in the United States and around the world may be determined far more than most of us realize by what American Christianity does about the race issue within the next few years.

15 Myrdal, *ibid.*, I, 1022.

CHAPTER FOUR

Desegregation and Integration

There is needed not only a clearer understanding of the difference between and the relation of separation and segregation, discussed in the preceding chapter, but also of desegregation and integration. The latter terms are closely related, but they should not be equated with each other.

Desegregation Versus Integration

In the fall of 1957, Hobart M. Corning, superintendent of the Washington, D.C., schools, stated: "Desegregation in Washington schools is 'complete as of today,' but integration is still to be accomplished." He correctly suggested that there was and is a difference between desegregation and integration. Liston Pope has said that integration "has a more positive content than the term desegregation."[1] Integration involves more than the removal of barriers and the elimination of compulsory segregation. This may be accomplished by desegregation. The latter is legal and more or less formal. Integration is voluntary and social. This means that integration is a much slower process than desegregation.

This is true even if we interpret "integration" in the broadest or loosest terms to refer to the mixing of the races in the schools and elsewhere. Many biracial communities in the South could desegregate their schools completely, as some have, and yet have comparatively

[1] *The Kingdom Beyond Caste*, p. 82.

little mixing of the races in those schools. The Negroes in the towns and cities of the South, as is also true in the urban centers of the North, usually live, by choice or compulsion, in distinctly Negro neighborhoods. This means that the vast majority of Negro pupils would continue to attend exclusively or predominantly Negro schools. Hodding Carter, following the Supreme Court decision, said that even if every Southern Negro child went that fall (1954) to the nearest school, without any restriction as to race, it was estimated that no more than one in four would be in a formerly all-white classroom. If the "freedom of choice" plan was followed as in Baltimore,[2] or if children had considerable freedom to transfer from one school district to another as in Louisville,[3] there would be, at least for the present, a further reduction in the amount of mixing in the schools.

Integration in the strictest sense involves a great deal more than the mere mixing of the races. There might be a great deal of this mixing with little if any true integration. In the deepest sense, integration has taken place only when those of another race or class are accepted as full and equal partners in a common task. It is based on mutual respect and on a sense of the dignity and worth of the human person. There must be a sharing with one another in the life of the community, whether that community is the school or the broader neighborhood. It is easily seen that desegregation is an essential prerequisite to the process of integration. There can be no meaningful sharing unless the barriers to contact and fellowship are removed. Their removal can be achieved through the process of desegregation.

Desegregation of the schools or of community life in general may or may not lead to genuine integration. Whether it does or does not will depend on the attitude of white and Negro people toward one another. The area of attitudes is the province of the Christian religion. It is becoming increasingly clear that there can be no real integration without the application of the Christian spirit to the relation of races.

[2] For a study of the Baltimore plan, see the booklet by Elinor Pancoast, *et al.*, *The Report of a Study on Desegregation in the Baltimore City Schools* (Baltimore, the Baltimore Commission on Human Relations, 1956).

[3] See Omer Carmichael and Weldon James, *The Louisville Story* (New York, Simon and Schuster, 1957).

Furthermore, it is very doubtful if there can be successful desegregation without considerable integration with or acceptance of those of the minority race by the majority. Desegregation without at least some attempt at and progress toward integration might make the general racial situation worse instead of better. It might add to the burdens and the frustrations of the minority group. All of this correctly suggests that the effectiveness even of desegregation can be measured largely by how much the Christian spirit has permeated the lives of those involved in the contemporary racial controversy.

Does this mean that legislation is meaningless or unwise in this whole area? There are some who argue that since segregation and desegregation are primarily "social," involving inner attitudes and motives, the legislative approach is entirely ineffective. Some say, "You cannot enforce morality by law," and incidentally thereby tacitly admit that the race problem is a moral issue. Now, what should be our attitude toward the legal and legislative approach to the problem of race relations? Segregation that is maintained by law can be repealed by law, although as a real achievement desegregation requires more than the mere passing of a law. A law or the repeal of a law, however, may provide the basis for and give support to moral action. It may maintain pressure toward a desired end.

After all, desegregation as such is not directly concerned with inner attitudes and purposes. It cannot and does not attempt to eliminate prejudice. It is concerned with the removal of injustice. Prejudice is a problem for the school and the church. Injustice is a legal matter, and hence its correction is the responsibility of the state.

Many people even if they understand the difference between desegregation and integration would still oppose desegregation. It is also true that the whole idea is frequently brushed aside by such statements as: "The people are not ready," or, "The Negroes do not want desegregation; the present disturbance is the work of Northern agitators and the NAACP." However, the strongest argument against desegregation, or at least the one that arouses the most prejudice, is, "It will lead to the mongrelizing of the races." This argument implies the inferiority of the Negro. In the final analysis most of the arguments against desegregation can be reduced to a conviction, conscious or unconscious, that the Negro is innately inferior. Whatever may be the reasons for opposition to compliance with the desegregation order of the Supreme Court, that opposition is very strong in many sections of the South.

In this connection it might be wise to examine again what the Court's decision actually covered. Did it and does it require the mixing of the races in the schools? The statement by the three-judge district court that handled the Clarendon County, South Carolina, case after the Supreme Court's decision has been rather widely quoted. The court said

. . . that the Supreme Court had not decided that the States must mix persons of different races. . . . What it has decided . . . is that a state may not deny to any person on account of race the right to attend any school that it maintains. . . . If the schools which it maintains are open to children of all races, no violation of the Constitution is involved even though the children of different races voluntarily attend different schools, as they attend different churches.

Some question might be raised about the word "voluntarily." If Negro children were "voluntarily" to attend Negro schools because of pressure or fear, then the spirit of the constitutional provision and of the Supreme Court decision would be violated.

The district court further said:

Nothing in the Constitution or the decision of the Supreme Court takes away from the people freedom to choose the schools they attend. The Constitution, in other words, does not require integration. It merely forbids discrimination.

The decision evidently was not intended to require the arbitrary mixing of the races in schools. It did and does call for the repeal of all legal segregation. The arbitrary mixing of races might violate the right of individual choice as much as forced segregation. Some force, if by force we mean law and the courts' intepretation of the law, may be necessary to change long-established customs, but there should be a minimum of force and the maintenance of a maximum of individual freedom in the present program of desegregation. Notice the expression "the maximum of individual freedom." This implies that there may have to be some limitation of freedom. Really, the state cannot provide for the freedom of all without at the same time limiting the freedom of all. The amount of limitation, potential or real, will depend on how much individuals would interfere with the freedom of others, freedom that is guaranteed by the government.

Desegregation: Progress and Problems

Since the Supreme Court's decision, considerable progress has been made toward the desegregation of the public schools in some states. Most of this progress, however, has been in the border states or the states with "a southern exposure." It is generally agreed that most of the easy territory has been desegregated; additional progress is going to be slow. The strategy of desegregation leaders apparently is to attempt desegregation in the spots where the resistance will be the weakest and to work gradually into the more difficult sections: in other words, to work from the circumference to the center.

An evidence of this is the fact that 634 of the 790 school districts that had desegregated by the fall of 1958 were in five states—Kentucky, Maryland, Missouri, Oklahoma, and West Virginia. All of these states, which have taken a positive position favorable to desegregation, are on the fringe of the South. Of the remaining 156 districts that had desegregated, 124 were in Texas, which belongs as much to the West as to the South; 17 in Delaware, which is more Southern than most people realize but certainly far removed from the Deep South; 8 in Arkansas; 3 in Tennessee; 3 in North Carolina; and the other the District of Columbia. That means that seven states— Florida and Virginia and the five states of the Deep South: South Carolina, Georgia, Alabama, Mississippi, and Louisiana—so far had no desegregated school districts, although Virginia has been under considerable pressure during the fall of 1958.*

It is no mere accident that the states of the Deep South, which are frequently classified as the defiant states, are the ones with the largest percentage of Negro school enrollment: Mississippi, 49.4 per cent; South Carolina, 42.8 per cent; Louisiana, 37.5 per cent; Alabama, 37.0 per cent; and Georgia, 31.6 per cent. It is these states along with the states of the Upper South that have passed many bills in an attempt to evade or nullify the Supreme Court decision or at least to delay compliance with it. In the first three months alone of 1956 the legislatures of five states—Alabama, Georgia, Mississippi, South Carolina, and Virginia—adopted at least forty-two prosegregation or antidesegregation measures. The *Southern School News* reports that a total of 196 segregation laws have been passed by the legislatures of eleven Southern states.

Laws passed by the different states have included such measures as the withholding of state funds from integrated schools, the repeal of compulsory-attendance laws, the provision of some type of pupil placement, and, as a last resort, authority to close the public schools. Other laws have been passed that would punish those who attend or teach in mixed schools and even revoke the licenses of teachers who support or condone such teaching. An indirect approach has been made through laws that would curb the National Association for the Advancement of Colored People (NAACP). Many of the laws passed by the various state legislatures will have to be tested in the courts, which may entail years of litigation. This in turn may delay desegregation, in some sections, for many years. This is one purpose of some of the laws.

There have been a number of other procedures, legislative and otherwise, that have been and are being used to preserve segregation. One of the most interesting and, in a sense, inconsistent is the insist-

* By February of 1959 the "massive resistance" program of Virginia began to break down. Several schools in three or four communities had reopened on a desegregated basis. There was evidence that others would follow, particularly in the Fall of 1959.

ence that the segregation question be dealt with on the state level and not on the local community level. This is interesting and inconsistent because it is being done by many of the people who are the most insistent on states' rights in contrast to federal authority. If they were entirely consistent they would defend the right of local communities to make their own decisions regarding desegregation. But they evidently fear any breach in the dike. To give anywhere might mean real danger everywhere. The result is that in some states, particularly in the states rather sharply divided in sentiment, the more vocal groups from the more strongly prosegregation section or sections of the state are forcing their views on the state as a whole and on communities in the state that could and would desegregate their schools peacefully if permitted to do so.

Recently there has been a tendency for previously moderate states to move into the resistance camp. This has been true in particular of Arkansas, Florida, North Carolina, and Virginia, and to a less degree of Texas. The hard-core states of the Deep South have tended to solidify their position, which is to evade the Supreme Court decision if possible, to defy it if necessary.

In the Deep South as elsewhere there is less resistance, with some striking exceptions, to desegregation in the larger cities than in the towns and the open country. In the border states, for example, desegregation began in the population centers: Baltimore, Louisville, and St. Louis. This was true although those cities contained a relatively large Negro population. For example, two-thirds of all Negroes in Missouri live in St. Louis and Kansas City, with 35 per cent of the public school pupils in St. Louis, Negro; 60 per cent of all the Negroes of Maryland live in Baltimore, with 35 per cent of the public school pupils, Negro; Wilmington has more than a third of all the Negroes in Delaware and 29 per cent of the public school enrollment is Negro; while Louisville has 28 per cent of the Negro population of Kentucky and 26 per cent of its public school enrollment is Negro. These cities have a larger percentage of their public school enrollment Negro than many of the larger cities in the Deep South. Incidentally, the school enrollment of Washington, D.C., for the fall of 1957 was 71.2

per cent Negro. The seemingly better chance for desegregation in urban communities doubtlessly explains the fact that most of the court cases in the South, since the Supreme Court's decision, have involved urban centers: Dallas, Little Rock, Miami, Nashville, New Orleans, Norfolk, and others.

Why does desegregation have a better chance in the cities, even when a large percentage of their public school pupils are Negro? One reason is that the people in larger cities are more cosmopolitan in their outlook. Also, there has been more integration of the Negro into various aspects of community life. Edgar L. Jones suggests[4] some additional factors that may make it easier in metropolitan areas to carry out a school desegregation program. Among those factors are the following:

(1) The obvious fact "that big-city dwellers by and large are not close to policy-making decisions. They . . . are generally resigned to the belief that there is little use trying to 'fight City Hall.' "

(2) "Another factor of urban life that could have a bearing on school desegregation is the equal status of white and Negro workers existing in some fields of employment as color lines have broken down." It is doubtful if this is very marked in most Southern cities.

(3) A third factor is the presence in many cities "of groups working for the promotion of racial harmony or improvement of the status of Negroes." Many of these groups have a Christian motivation and draw much of their leadership from the churches. Many of the churches, along with their ministers, must be included in the groups or organizations working for better human relations.

(4) Another factor providing an environment in cities that is frequently more favorable to desegregation than in the towns, villages, and the open country is the amount of residential segregation.

There are notable exceptions to the last suggestion but, generally speaking, because of residential segregation or separation, the desegregation of schools in many Southern cities would affect a relatively small number of Negro pupils and comparatively few schools, white or Negro. For example, in Oklahoma City two years of desegrega-

4 Shoemaker, *With All Deliberate Speed*, pp. 75–80.

tion led to the mixing of the races in only ten schools, located mostly in fringe areas. Less than 7 per cent of white pupils and approximately 15 per cent of the colored were affected. In Tulsa, in the second year of desegregation, only 110 of the city's 4,500 Negro pupils were enrolled in formerly all-white schools.

As one would expect, the strongest resistance to desegregation is found in what is termed the Black Belt, a section mostly in the Deep South, where the Negroes outnumber the white people. Parenthetically, the counties with more Negroes than white people decreased from 286 in 1900 to 180 in 1940, with a further decrease since that time. Resistance organizations, such as the White Citizens' Councils, are strongest in the Black Belt. The white people of this area, along with scattered extremists from other sections, have maintained rather consistently the initiative in the present racial controversy. It would be unrealistic not to recognize the very grave problems faced by counties and communities in the Black Belt and frankly to admit that it will be a long time before desegregation can be expected in the region.

Desegregation: Plans and Prospects

Some local school boards in Southern states have perfected plans for gradual compliance with the Supreme Court's decree. These plans usually follow one of two processes: (1) from the top down, beginning with the senior high school, or (2) from the bottom up, beginning with the elementary grades.

An example of the first plan was the one worked out by the Little Rock school board and approved by the federal courts. It proposed to start on the senior high school level, to be followed by the junior high schools, and lastly the elementary schools. The entire program was set up to cover six years. An example of the second plan was the one started by Nashville in the fall of 1957. It began with the first grade. A plan submitted by Hopkins County, Kentucky, to desegregate one grade at a time, taking twelve years to complete the process, was not held by the courts to satisfy the Supreme Court's requirement of "all deliberate speed."

In contrast to communities that have followed a program of gradual desegregation, other places have undertaken the complete desegregating of the school system at one time. There is considerable difference of opinion about which is the wiser procedure. Some difficult things are best done slowly, while in the case of others it would be wiser to do them quickly. For example, it would be foolish to try to climb a steep and dangerous mountain by starting off as fast as one could go. On the other hand, it would be equally foolish for one to try to quit heavy drinking by tapering off. Is segregation a mountain to be climbed or a bad habit to be broken? It is possible that it has some of the characteristics of both, and hence both methods may be justifiably used.

There is some evidence that there is less likelihood of conflict and unfriendly relations when the entire school system is desegregated at one time. At least what happened in Louisville, Baltimore, and Washington was in rather marked contrast to what happened in Little Rock, Nashville, and other Southern communities. However, there were several factors that explained or helped to explain the relative smoothness and success in the former cities as compared to the difficulties and conflict in the latter.

Desegregation with a minimum of disturbance depends primarily upon the following: (1) A clear and unequivocal statement of policy by leaders with prestige and authority. (2) A firm enforcement of the changed policy by the authorities even in the face of initial resistance. (3) A willingness to resort to law and strong enforcement policies when necessary to deal with actual or attempted violations or incitement to violation of the new policy. (4) An appeal to the individuals concerned in terms of their religious convictions and their acceptance of American ideals.[5]

Another factor which seems to be of major importance is adequate community preparation. This quite evidently was one secret to the apparent success of desegregation in Louisville and Baltimore.

[5] See Kenneth B. Clark, "Some Problems Related to the Problem of Desegregation," *The Journal of Negro Education*, XXIII, No. 3 (Summer, 1954), pp. 341ff.

A very real problem that has been faced by communities that have desegregated has been the difference in the educational level of Negro and white pupils. On the average, the Negro youngsters are considerably behind the white pupils. This condition, as suggested formerly, may be an indictment against segregated schools and the separate-but-equal doctrine.

The answer to the problem of the Negro child's educational lag seems to be something similar to the three-track curriculum of St. Louis or the four-track plan worked out by the Washington, D.C., schools. These plans are not a great deal different from those used already in many school systems. The St. Louis plan provides separate classes for the bright, the average, and the slow students. There will be, in most cases, a larger percentage of Negro students, at least for the time being, in the classes for slow students and fewer in the other sections. For example, in Washington there were 158 white and 1,319 Negro students in a "basic" course for slow learners, in contrast to 315 white and only 50 Negro students in a college preparatory course.

Another problem that may be created by desegregation is the loss of employment by Negro schoolteachers. Teaching has been one of the best employment opportunities for better educated Negroes. *Southern School News* reveals that approximately 300 Negro teachers in Oklahoma have lost their jobs, with about 60 in Kentucky, 58 in West Virginia, 20 in Missouri, and about 20 in Texas. In some of the city systems, such as St. Louis, Baltimore, and Washington, there has been little if any displacement.

As we face the resistance to desegregation and the many problems it posits for whites and Negroes, let us ask again what will be the ultimate fate of the Supreme Court decision in the South. Virginius Dabney recently reported that the Gallup Poll found that two-thirds of those canvassed in the South disapproved the Court's ruling. By contrast, two-thirds of those in the rest of the country approved the ruling. He then said that all of this raises a question as to the implication of such a situation for the South. He asked the pointed question, "How long can the South afford to remain in flat and violent disagreement with the North and West on so fundamental an issue as race relations?"

The people of the South are, in the main, quite conservative. They are slow to change, and particularly resent and will resist a "dictated change" from outside the region. Their conservatism also leads them, in the main, to recoil from the use of extreme measures. Thus, their conservatism may be both an asset and a hindrance to desegregation. It will be a hindrance to immediate desegregation, but it may, in the long run, contribute to the attainment of desegregation.

It now seems that the ultimate fate in the South of the Supreme Court decree will rest with the great group of Southern people who do not want desegregation; they will use every legal resort to evade and delay it, and yet they "deplore racism and rabble rousing, and fear violence."[6] And it might have been added that many of that great middle group of Southerners respect the Constitution and want to be law-abiding citizens. They recognize the need for and the inevitability of change, but they dread to break with the past. Some of them are intersectional and even international in perspective, and yet emotionally they are Southerners, and in some cases Georgians, Mississippians, or Virginians. For many of them there is terrific inner tension. This is difficult for one to understand who does not live with the conflict. This tension, however, is one of the main hopes for progress toward desegregation. Something must be done, sooner or later, to release tension if one is to continue to live with it.

Integration and Intermarriage

Many people tend to equate integration and amalgamation. They argue that we cannot have the former without its inevitably leading to the latter. And since many of them confuse desegregation and integration, they use the fear of intermarriage and amalgamation as an argument against and a block to desegregation. Incidentally, there can be and has been a great deal of amalgamation without intermarriage. The whole sex fear, which Hodding Carter says is "a

[6] Milton L. Barron (ed.), *American Minorities* (New York, Knopf, 1957), p. 222.

powerful emotional block to clear thought and constructive action in the field of race," plays "an almost demonic role in the American culture conflict."[7]

Regardless of the source or strength of the fear of intermarriage and amalgamation, which is so prevalent among the people of the South, there are many politicians and even some so-called religious leaders who are seeking to capitalize on this concern and confusion. This strategy, which is an appeal to prejudice, has been used effectively in the fight against the implementation of the Supreme Court's decision concerning school segregation. Many of the opponents of the Supreme Court order have claimed that there cannot be mixing in the classroom without resulting intermarriage. Some even claim that the movement for desegregation is an effort to mongrelize the race, and that it is a communist plot to undermine and to overthrow our nation.

If people were not so prejudiced, and hence could think straight, they would realize how unfounded are most of the fears regarding intermarriage. They would understand that there could be desegregation of the public schools with comparatively little mixing of the races. Actually, according to *Southern School News*, only 2,892 of the 8,677 school districts in the Southern region contain any Negro scholastics. There are only seven states in the South where every school district is biracial. They are Alabama, Florida, Louisiana, Mississippi, North Carolina, South Carolina, and Virginia. Not only do many school districts fail to have any Negro people, but many of the 2,892 that do have, including most of the 790 of this number that had desegregated by the fall of 1958, have comparatively few Negro scholastics.

But what of mixing of the races in the schools? Will it inevitably lead to considerable intermarriage? If white children go to school with Negro children will they marry Negro young people? These questions when asked by some people are the tools of a prejudiced mind rather than the inquiry of an open mind. There are others,

[7] Buell G. Gallagher, *Color and Conscience: The Irrepressible Conflict* (New York, Harper, 1946), p. 161.

however, who are asking these questions honestly. Some of the questions of the latter, however, may stem from a conviction, possibly unrecognized or unacknowledged, that the Negro is innately inferior.

As suggested previously, there can be desegregation with little if any integration. However, small children are relatively free from prejudice and they will naturally tend to accept those of other races into the life and activities of the group. But there still remains the question, quite perplexing and disturbing to some people, Will all of this lead to intermarriage?

In fairness, it should be said that mixing in the schools might lead to some intermarriage, but very little if we are to judge by what has happened where there is and has been no legal segregation. For example, there is little intermarriage in the North, although there are no laws against it and although Negro children are free to go to school with white children. There is plenty of evidence that "barriers of the mind have never needed to be sustained by barriers of law."[8] There are some deep-set barriers of the mind against intermarriage of Negroes and white people.

In an article based on a doctoral dissertation, a Catholic author reveals that a study of over 100,000 marriage licenses in Washington, D.C., disclosed 375 interracial marriages over an eight-year period, with only 26 of those Negro-white marriages. A spot comparison showed a considerable decrease in the number of Negro-white marriages over a twenty-year period. For example, there were twelve Negro-white marriages in 1927, as compared to six in 1947. Damon P. Young, in a master's thesis at Howard University, said: "Intermarriage in the District of Columbia is almost a social monstrosity at the present time." A study of Boston, with its abolitionist heritage, covering the years 1914–1938, revealed that only thirteen of ten thousand white people married Negroes. The number of interracial marriages "is an inconsequential dribble in the annual stream of American wedlock . . . a microscopic percentage of the total."[9]

Not only has there been a decrease in the number of Negro-white

[8] Ashmore, *An Epitaph for Dixie*, p. 61.
[9] Gallagher, *op. cit.*, p. 167.

marriages but there also appears to be a decrease in extramarital interracial sex relations. One possible reason for this is the progress the Negro has made and his accompanying greater racial pride. This suggests that improved education for the Negro would decrease rather than increase the frequency either of sex relations with whites outside marriage or of intermarriage with them. Of the comparatively few Negro-white marriages at the present time, most of them are among the lower economic classes, frequently involving eccentrics or white women of foreign ancestry.

If we use the fear of intermarriage as an argument against desegregation, it implies that we would not want our son or daughter to go to school with anyone we did not want them to marry. Does this mean that we would defend segregation on this basis? Let us consider what that would logically mean. Most of us would not want a son or daughter of ours to marry a non-Christian; therefore, non-Christians should not be permitted to go to school with them. Some of us would not want our children to marry one of another religious faith. We would not want our children to cross over a number of racial lines when they marry, and we even believe they should give serious consideration to the general family, social, and economic background of a prospective mate. Would we have segregated schools for all the various groups with whom we would not want our children to intermarry? If carried to its ridiculous conclusion, then we would have a school just for our little Mary or Johnny and the few to whom we would be willing for them to be married.

Is it not true that the intermarriage scare is applied only to the Negro? Are the opponents of desegregation being entirely fair at this point? We may be strongly opposed to desegregation, and there may be some defensible arguments against immediate desegregation in some places, but will you not agree that we need a better argument than the fear of intermarriage?

Some people seem to think that all Negroes, particularly Negro men, want to marry into the white race. Strange as it may seem, some of the individuals who are most positive that the Negro men want to marry white wives will justify segregation with the argument:

"Negroes want to be separate. They do not want to mix with white people. They would be perfectly happy if the agitators would leave them alone." Such reasoning is inconsistent for one who uses the fear of intermarriage as a defense of segregation. Myrdal in his study found that the Negro's main concern was with economic discrimination, and that intermarriage was "of rather distant and doubtful interest."[10]

R. R. Moton, former president of Tuskegee Institute, said some years ago that Negroes theoretically would defend the right of freedom of choice in marriage, but that practically they resented the action of the few individuals of the race who crossed over the color line for marriage partners. He concluded, "To the race as a whole it constitutes active disloyalty to the Negro race."[11]

Roi Ottley, another Negro, agrees with Myrdal and Moton. He says: "Negroes do not struggle for equal rights to marry white women. . . . Essentially the masses of Negroes are concerned only with jobs—for they believe that fundamentally their problem is an economic one."[12] There is rather general agreement among Negroes and whites, both North and South, that intermarriage is not desirable.

There are one or two other things that should be said about intermarriage in general. First, there is, and has been through the years, considerable sexual intermingling of the races. The great number of mulattoes is an evidence of this fact. One source says there were nearly 600,000 mulattoes among somewhat less than 4.5 million Negroes in the United States in 1860. Most of these resulted from the sex relations of white men with Negro women.

Owing not only to the relations of white men with Negro women but also to the intermingling of mulattoes with pure Negroes, the proportion of mulattoes has continued to increase. It is estimated that the proportion doubled from 1850 to 1910. In 1850, according to the United States census, one Negro in nine was classified as

10 Myrdal, *An American Dilemma*, I, 61.
11 R. R. Moton, *What the Negro Thinks* (New York, Doubleday, Doran, 1929), p. 241.
12 Roi Ottley, *New World A-Coming* (Boston, Houghton Mifflin, 1943), p. 346.

mulatto. This had increased to one in five in 1910. The Census Bureau came to the conclusion that the distinction between black and mulatto was of little value, and dropped it after 1920.

No one can know the amount of mixing, but Myrdal says that "the great majority of American Negroes are not of pure African descent."[13] The study most frequently quoted, which doubtlessly is as reliable as any available, suggests that only 22 per cent of Negroes are of pure African ancestry. All the others are mixed with white or Indian blood or both, with 51 per cent of the total of white and Negro ancestry. Some classified as "Negro" are biologically white but legally and sociologically Negro. Some, but no one knows how many, of those who are biologically white pass each year into the ranks of the white people. While it seems evident that there is not as much mixing as in recent years, there continues to be some. A South African writer, after a study of the race problem in the United States as well as in other countries of the West, concluded that miscegenation was far more common in the South where there were laws against intermarriage than in the North where there are no such laws.

The preceding at least points out that the real issue in the contemporary discussion is not a choice between segregation with racial purity and desegregation and integration with amalgamation and intermarriage.

All of the mixing of the races through the years, which continues at least to some degree in our day, makes one wonder if the white man is primarily concerned with "the purity of the race," which Gallagher says is a hallucination in the United States,[14] or with the legalizing of the relationship. There seems to be a difference between the talk and the behavior of some Southern white men. Some who loudly support the color line may quietly condone sex relations between the males of the dominant group and the females of the subordinate group.

Another thing that should be considered in discussing intermar-

---

[13] *Op. cit.*, I, 106.
[14] *Op. cit.*, p. 165.

riage is the fact that "it takes two to make a match." Every Negro-white marriage involves a white person as well as a Negro. Why put all or most of the blame on the Negro?

What should be our conclusion concerning intermarriage? Is the marriage of Negroes and whites wise or unwise? It is definitely not good common sense, in our culture, for a Negro and a white person to marry. This is just as true for the Negro as for the white person. And we might add that if such a marriage, or any other marriage, hurts the cause of Christ, then it becomes positively wrong or sinful for a Christian. Marriage for a child of God is not exclusively a personal matter. He should consider its effects on his family, his community, his church, and on the kingdom of God in general.

However, our objection to Negro-white marriages should not be because we consider the Negro innately inferior. We do not believe that many other mixed marriages—racial or religious—are wise. In these cases, in the main, our opposition is not based on any idea of superiority or inferiority, but on the welfare of the persons involved and on their difficulty in attaining a satisfactory marriage relationship. Particular consideration should always be given to any children who might be born into such a home.

Although we do not believe it is wise for Negroes and whites to marry, we do believe that the Scriptures have been misinterpreted and are being wrongly applied by some people during the present controversy regarding desegregation, integration, and intermarriage. Many people are searching for "divine approval" for their particular position on the segregation issue. All of us need to be careful that we do not twist the Scriptures to support our particular position. Some of the opponents of desegregation lay great stress on the laws and regulations in the Old Testament concerning intermarriage. For them, of course, an argument against intermarriage is an argument against desegregation.

Although the question of intermarriage, as we have tried to prove, really does not belong in the controversy concerning school desegregation, let us examine briefly the biblical restrictions concerning intermarriage. The general emphasis of the Jews was against intermarriage.

In the Pentateuch (Ex. 34:12–16; Deut. 7:1–8), seven nations are listed, all in the territory given to Israel by the Lord, to whom God's people were not to give their sons and daughters in marriage. The restrictions concerning intermarriage here and elsewhere in the Old Testament were primarily national or tribal and not racial. Furthermore, the main motive for the restrictions was religious. The following from Deuteronomy pointedly sets forth this motive: "You shall not make marriages with them, giving your daughters to their sons or taking their daughters for your sons. For they would turn away your sons from following me, to serve other gods" (Deut. 7:3–4). Notice particularly the last sentence.

The scholars generally agree that the prohibitions against intermarriage throughout the entire Old Testament were primarily and almost exclusively based on religious grounds. For example, Epstein says that the prohibition against intermarriage with the seven nations in Deuteronomy (7:1–5) "was partly political but mainly religious";[15] while David Mace suggests that the motive for the later compaign of Ezra and Nehemiah "to establish racial endogamy is quite clear. It is the fear of idolatry creeping into the national life."[16]

There may be valid arguments against interracial marriages, but let us not use the Bible to support such a position. Some current talk about God being the first segregationist either stems from a confusion of separation and segregation or it is sacrilegious and approaches blasphemy. The prohibitions concerning mixed marriages in the Bible might be used to argue against the marriage of a Christian and a non-Christian and conceivably against some interfaith marriages, but they cannot legitimately be used to support arguments against racial intermarriage. Let all of us "rightly divide the word of truth."

[15] L. M. Epstein, *Marriage Laws in the Bible and the Talmud* (Cambridge, Harvard, 1942), p. 158.
[16] David R. Mace, *Hebrew Marriage: A Sociological Study* (London, Epworth Press, 1953), p. 148.

CHAPTER FIVE

Biblical Teachings and Segregation

The Bible in various ways has been brought into the contemporary controversy concerning segregation and desegregation. It has been used to defend every conceivable position. This has been done although there is little material in the Bible directly related to race relations in general or to racial segregation in particular.

The preceding does not mean, however, that there is nothing of significance in the Bible on race and race relations. There is an abundance of teachings and principles, ideas and ideals that are relevant to the contemporary racial situation. Those principles or ideals are an integral part of the very heart of the biblical message. To deny them and their relevance to contemporary life is to deny the gospel itself. In this chapter we shall attempt to set out briefly some of the basic biblical concepts that may properly be applied to the race problem and to the segregation-desegregation issue.[1]

[1] For a fuller discussion, see my book *The Bible and Race* (Nashville, Broadman Press, 1959) and Everett Tilson, *Segregation and the Bible* (New York, Abingdon Press, 1958). The former is primarily an exposition of pertinent biblical passages. The latter is a more general discussion, giving considerable attention to arguments, based on the Bible, by both segregationists and desegregationists.

The Nature of God

The proper beginning place for a study of the teachings of the Bible on segregation, or on any other issue, is its teachings concerning God. He is the point of reference in the Christian religion. He is the source of authority in Christian theology and in Christian ethics. For example, in the latter the final determinant of right and wrong is in the will of God. That will is revealed, however, not only by what God says but also and basically by what he is. His will is grounded in his nature. If we want to know God's will for us in the area of race relations—and surely every sincere Christian wants to know—let us begin with a study of the nature of God as we find it revealed in the Bible.

The first thing that impresses us about the God revealed in the Bible is that he is a Person. He has all the qualities that are essential to personality: the power to think, to judge, to feel, to will, to communicate. We discover that he is not only a Person but that he is a moral person. Really, one cannot be a person in the true sense without being a moral person. The God of the Bible is a god of holiness, righteousness, and justice. His moral character is portrayed in the Bible as dependable, as a constant among the uncertainties in human life and history.

The fact that God is a moral Person has significant implications for us in our relations to him and to our fellow man. Since he is a Person, our relations to him cannot be right unless they are right on a personal basis. While we should be faithful to the formal requirements of our religion, this faithfulness will not make us acceptable to God if we have left undone the weightier or the more important matters (see Matt. 23:23). Those weightier matters have to do with our relations to our fellow man. God expects us to treat others as he would treat them.

God, who is holy, righteous, just, and merciful, expects his children to possess the same qualities. His word through Moses to the people of Israel was, "You shall be holy; for I the Lord your God am holy" (Lev. 19:2). What is true of holiness is true of every other moral quality that God possesses. This fact has tremendous significance for race relations. God expects us to manifest his spirit, his attitude toward all men of all races.

Jesus directly related this whole idea to love for enemies. He said to his disciples, "Practice loving your enemies and praying for your persecutors." Why should they practice or continue to love their enemies? Jesus gives the answer as follows: "To prove that you are sons of your Father in heaven, for He makes His sun rise on bad as well as good people, and makes the rain come down on doers of right and wrong alike" (Matt. 5:44–45, Williams).

Jesus followed this statement with that abidingly challenging ideal: "So you, my followers, ought to be perfect, as your heavenly Father is." God's children should be like their Father in love and in perfection or maturity. Our lives are to be judged not by what others expect us to do but by what God expects us to be, and he expects us to be like him. What a challenging and humbling thought for all of us!

The God revealed in the Bible is not only a moral Person; he is also the Creator of all. There may be far more significance than most people realize in the fact that the first book of the Bible opens with the statement: "In the beginning God created the heavens and the earth." Everything is derived from God. The fact that God is creator of all is emphasized throughout the Bible but particularly in the latter portion of Isaiah. There God is revealed as "the Creator of the ends of the earth" (40:28); it was he

> who created the heavens and
>   stretched them out,
> who spread forth the earth and
>   what comes from it,
> who gives breath to the people upon it
>   and spirit to those who walk in it.
> [42:5]

He not only created the earth and all on the earth (45:12), but he was also the Creator of Israel (43:1) and hence of her king (43:15).

His sons and his daughters from the east and the west, from the north and the south have been created by him for his glory (43:5–7).

This emphasis on God as Creator is also found in the New Testament, with the additional emphasis that Jesus was a partner in that creative work (John 1:1–3). Paul says that "all things were created through him and for him" (Col. 1:16). The Christian believes that this creative work of God is a present reality as well as a past achievement.

Not only is God the creator of all, but the Bible plainly reveals that he is the ruler over all. What he has created he has the right and the power to control. Any limitations of his control are self-limitations. For example, he has given man freedom and man can limit God in what God can do in and through him. But it is very important to understand that final authority rests with God. He is the Lord of history. In the drama of life he is the chief actor, or possibly better, he is the author and the producer of the drama.

This biblical doctrine or concept of the sovereignty of God, of a God who not only has a will for the world but whose will ultimately will be done, is of major importance in the area of human relations. Some have misinterpreted the doctrine and have used it as a justification for inactivity. In other words, their viewpoint has been that God will be victorious, that he can achieve his purposes by himself, and hence he does not need or expect our help in achieving his will in the world. At best we may be interested spectators as the drama of history is unfolded before us.

There are others who more correctly believe that God expects his children to be participants with him in the unfolding drama or, to use biblical language, that he expects his children to be laborers together with him in achieving his purposes for the world. They also believe that their cooperation with God can help to determine whether his will is achieved early or late. They also are convinced that the longer his will is delayed, the greater will be the dislocation and suffering in human relations. This dislocation and suffering will continue until God's purposes in the world are achieved. Incidentally, man's activity or inactivity will not condition or determine whether or not God will be ultimately triumphant. His reign, his rule, his kingdom will come sooner or later. He is not only the beginning but also the end of the historic process.

Such a faith in the final victory of God among men, in every area of life, should be and will be a mighty motivating force in the life of an understanding, sincere child of God. If he has a conviction that he is within the will of God he will be willing to face opposition, ridicule, and persecution. He will do this with a deep conviction that he is on the side that will ultimately win. It is this spirit and this motivation that have given to the world her pioneering prophetic spirits, who have blazed new moral and spiritual trails for God and for mankind.

It is also the conviction of the child of God that God cannot be ruler of all unless he is sovereign over all. This means that the God revealed in the Bible cannot be limited in his interest or activity to one or two restricted segments of life. The God who created the heavens and the earth is concerned about everything in the heavens and on the earth.

This means, among other things, that God has a will concerning every area of human relations. The Sunday-school teacher who said, "I do not see how being a Christian has anything to do with my relations to the Negroes," had not only a very limited conception of the Christian life but also a very distorted view of the nature of the sovereign God of the universe.

This sovereign God of the universe, who is creatively active in the life of the world and who exercises dynamic control over the world, is revealed in the Bible as Father. This idea of God as Father is found in the Old Testament (see Deut. 32:6; Isa. 63:16; 64:8; Jer. 3:19), but it is particularly prevalent in the life and ministry of Jesus. The emphasis on the fatherhood of God was one of the most distinctive elements in the teachings of Jesus. He gave to the idea new depth and meaning. "He enriched it beyond recognition."[2]

Jesus referred to God as "the Father," "my Father," "your Father,"

2 James S. Stewart, *The Life and Teaching of Jesus Christ* (London, SCM Press, 1952), p. 81.

and in the Model Prayer as "Our Father." All of these usages are of real importance to the Christian, but "Our Father" is particularly significant for us in the study of segregation and desegregation.

Luke tells us that as Jesus prayed one of his disciples asked him, "Lord, teach us to pray" (Luke 11:1). If we could hear him pray, would not the disciple's question be a natural one for us to ask? If we could hear him pray we would realize that we need to know how to pray. We certainly need to understand the inclusiveness of genuine prayer. We need to comprehend the full significance of the first two words of the prayer Jesus taught his disciples.

When we pray "Our Father," we should remember that every other man and woman, boy and girl in the world who has been brought into union with God through faith in Christ can likewise pray, "Our Father." Are we broad enough, big enough, Christian enough to include them within the circle of our prayer? This may not be much of a problem if they are on some mission field, but what if they live down the street, across the tracks, in shantytown? What if their skins are red, yellow, or black: can we still pray with them, "Our Father"? If we cannot, then we have failed to catch the spirit of our Father and their Father; we are not acting like members of the family of God.

Georgia Harkness says that it is time that we quit talking so much about God as Father and began acting as if he really was our Father and as if we were brothers. She further says that this "would be about the most revolutionary thing that could happen to our society."[3] There is no place where this idea or these ideas would be more revolutionary than in the area of race relations.

The Nature of Man

Not only does the biblical conception of God but also that of man have major significance in the realm of race relations. This has been implied in what has been said previously.

What does the Bible reveal concerning the nature of man? Again,

[3] Georgia Harkness, *The Modern Rival of Christian Faith: An Analysis of Secularism* (New York, Abingdon-Cokesbury, 1952), p. 192.

we shall not attempt to set out the entire biblical doctrine or estimate of man. We shall limit ourselves to those few ideas that are most
pertinent to our discussion.

The Bible clearly reveals that all peoples are from one family
stock. Back of every race of men is the human race, which gives unity
to all. This concept of the unity of the human race is basic in the Old
Testament. This is true whether one goes back to the creation story
for the beginning of human life or to the story of Noah and his family
as the source of the races of mankind.

Paul, in his sermon on Mars Hill, set out pointedly this concept of
the oneness of the human family. He said that God "made of one
["from one" RSV] every nation of men to dwell on all the face of
the earth" (Acts 17:26 ASV). There are different interpretations
of the meaning of the two words "of one," some interpreting "One"
to refer to God, while others—the majority of commentators—make
it refer to one source or family. Williams and Phillips both translate
the expression "from one forefather."

Regardless of which idea is correct, Paul stressed in his sermon the
oneness of God and the unity of mankind. What a long way we
would go in solving our problems concerning race and settling our
disputes concerning segregation and desegregation, if we simply
accepted men and women as members of the human family rather
than as members of a particular race, class, or caste!

Add to the preceding the fact that all Christians are in the spiritual
family of God, have been redeemed by the blood of Christ, and have
been brought into union with him, and we lay the foundation for
the solution of all problems of human relations. How can any child
of God, when he considers all these things, justify or defend his
prejudice and discrimination against any man because of his class
or color?

Another concept in the biblical view of man, of major importance
for us, is the fact that man was created in the image of God. Emil
Brunner says that "the whole Christian doctrine of man hangs upon
the interpretation of this expression."[4] If Brunner is correct, then it is

---

[4] *Man in Revolt* (Philadelphia, Westminster Press, 1947), p. 92.

very important that the expression be correctly interpreted. There have been and are varied meanings given to "the image." Central to any correct interpretation must be the idea of personality. God is a person; man is created a person. A person can think, judge, feel, and will, which involves freedom of choice. Possibly no one quality is more basic to personality, however, than the capacity and even the necessity for communication.

God created man in his own image; he created him as a person, as one with the capacity for communication with his fellow man but on the highest level with God himself. It is his capacity for fellowship with God that enables man to transcend nature, although in a sense he is a part of nature. Another way of stating the same thing is to say that the one thing that makes man most distinctly man is that he finds satisfaction in communication with God, and in a lesser sense in fellowship with his fellow man. The tragedy of sin is that it separates man from God, that it disrupts his communication with God and his fellowship with his fellow man.

The rather interesting thing is that man even in his fallen, sinful state does not lose entirely his hunger for communication with God. It is this eternally gnawing hunger that explains man's constant restlessness. He is searching for that which satisfies, although he may not know that he will find that satisfaction in God and in God alone. This restlessness is an indication that the image of God in man has not been completely destroyed, but rather marred or defaced. It awaits for its renewal the touch of the divine spirit at the time when through union with Christ the individual becomes a child of God. Looked at from the divine perspective, this all means that God is constantly seeking man, that he is redemptive in his purposes, that he is on a continuous, unceasing search for the lost.

Whatever may be the correct interpretation of the "image of God" in man and of the effects of sin on that image, there is no question concerning the import of the image for human relations in general and for race relations in particular. The image of God in man gives to man infinite worth and dignity. God himself, on at least one occasion, related directly the high value he placed on man with the fact that the latter was created in his image (Gen. 9:6).

The important thing for us to remember is that *all* are created in the image of God and that Christ died for all to restore that image, which had been marred by sin. This means that all should be treated with respect. No man who has been created in the image of God, no man for whom Christ died should ever be treated as a mere means or instrument, but always as an end of infinite value. This should be just as true of the Negro yardman or elevator operator as it is of one's husband or wife, one's son or daughter. One is created in the image of God just as much as the other. The life of one is just as precious in the sight of God as the other. Let us never forget, however, that it is because of man's relation to God that "Christianity . . . has asserted the sovereign worth of man."[5]

This sovereign worth of man, based on the fact that he was created in the image of God, makes democracy—both political and spiritual —possible and also necessary. Democracy is a necessity because man, although a creation of God, never completely escapes the temptation to usurp the place of God.[6] The white man, in the racial controversy, needs to guard against this ever present temptation. The thing that will save him from the temptation is to remember that he is equally a creature of God with the Negro, equally dependent upon God, and equally responsible to God.

The Christian, white or Negro, should recognize that although he may be influenced and limited by his environment he is not to be a slave to it. In the area of race as well as in every other realm we are responsible ultimately to the Creator and not to custom. God created us all morally responsible individuals, and we are accountable to him.

Another idea concerning the nature of man, which is quite relevant

[5] Ernest F. Scott, *Man and Society in the New Testament* (New York, Scribner's, 1946), p. 5.
[6] This emphasis is found in Reinhold Niebuhr, particularly in his *The Children of Light and the Children of Darkness* (New York, Scribner's, 1944).

to the segregation-desegregation issue, is the Christian position, maintained rather consistently, concerning human equality. The Christian conception of equality is closely related to the idea of the image of God in man. Really, the only sound basis for human equality is the fact that all men have been created by God and that all have been created in the image of God. On the other hand, it is just as difficult to defend the idea of basic human inequality if one believes that God is the creator of all and that he has created all men in his image. In other words, all men of every class and race are equally men and are treated with equal respect by God. In dealing with them he shows no partiality, he does not look on their outer conditions—the class they belong to, where they live, what they have, how much they know, or the color of their skins.

Certainly men are not created equal in abilities. What a drab world we would have if all men had the same abilities and to the same degree! Men, however, "are equal to one another in all that is involved in being a man."[7] They are equal in being although not in performance, equal in essence although unequal in capacity. They are all equally dependent on God.

This idea of equality is particularly important in the family of God. The only differences God recognizes in men is in their relation to him. Those who have come into the family of God through union with Christ are equally children of God, and can be assured that they are equally precious in the sight of God. This idea of the equality of all who have come into union with Christ is a central theme in the epistles of Paul (see 1 Cor. 12:12-20; Gal. 3:26-28; Eph. 2:13-16; Col. 3:11).

If all of us had a proper understanding of our relation to God as creator and ruler, we would see how foolish and irrelevant is the whole discussion of the supposed innate superiority and inferiority of races. In the presence of God, the creator and sustainer of all, there is no room either for haughty egotism or for a cringing sense of inferiority and defeat. In God's presence all are equal. All of this is doubly true of those who have come into the family of God through

[7] Francis J. Sheed, *Society and Sanity* (London, Sheed and Ward, 1953), p. 7.

union with Christ. They are children of the King. There is no partiality in his family.

The Work of Christ

We have already mentioned the work of Christ as Redeemer. It is the fact that Christ died for all men, along with the fact that they were created in the image of God, that makes man of more worth than all things material. In other words, his value is derivative; "it lies in *relatedness to God*." And we should not have to remind ourselves that Christ died for one man as much as for another. He knows no class or color line. His abiding invitation is, "Whosoever will may come." The only condition for coming is faith, and the way of faith is open to all men. Christ accepts all on the same basis.

He "has broken down the dividing wall of hostility" ("the barrier that kept us apart" Williams), not only between the Jew and the Gentile but also between all other groups that have let a wall or a barrier divide them. This he has done and will do by making us one or "one body" in him. When we become "one new man in place of two" there is unity instead of diversity and peace not only with God but also with one another.

The secret to peace with one another is our peace with God. By reconciling both Jew and Gentile to God, by bringing them into one body, which was accomplished through the cross, Christ brought hostility to an end (Eph. 2:16). This hostility could mean hostility to the law, but it might mean that he "has put a stop to hostility between us" (Williams). Whether or not the latter is a correct translation, it is a correct idea. We do need to remember, however, that what has been accomplished by Christ becomes a reality in human society only as we cooperate with him. If we will let him, he will make us one; he will remove the hostility that divides us into warring class and racial camps. "Race and national distinctions vanish in Christ."[8] And let us not forget that he is our only hope. He and he alone will bring peace with God and with our fellow man. All human

[8] A. T. Robertson, *Word Pictures in the New Testament* (Nashville, Broadman Press, 1931), IV, 526.

animosities will disappear as we are made one in him, who is the Prince of Peace.

A similar emphasis is found in that wonderful passage on the resurrected life in the Colossian letter (Col. 3:1–17). Paul tells the Colossians to put off the old nature and then admonishes them to put on the new nature or new self. He states that this new nature is being renewed or "is in the process of being made new" (Williams). Phillips translates the expression as follows: "The new man is out to learn what he ought to be." The renewal, in one sense, is a process. When we are brought into union with Christ we unfortunately bring into that experience many of the weaknesses and limitations of the old self. We need to maintain a constant process of education or of renewal "in knowledge." This knowledge, if it is to be most significant for us, must not be simply theoretical. It must become a living experience, a vital phase of our lives. It is doubtful if we really learn anything until we have expressed and verified it in life.

The end or goal of the Christian's knowledge, which is being constantly renewed, is the full realization or restoration of the image of the Creator. There is a sense, of course, in which the image is restored when we become children of God, when we are brought into union with Christ, who is the exact reproduction of the original image. But what child of God would dare to say that the original image has been completely restored in him? As we grow in our likeness to the One who gave his life to restore the image in us, we will grow in our likeness to the One who originally created us in his image. It was Paul who said that we "are being changed into his likeness from one degree of glory to another" (2 Cor. 3:18). The rapidity of the change depends on our cooperation with him. He will mold us more and more into his image or likeness, if we will let him.

Some conscientious Christians fail to see the relevance of all of this to human relations. Paul, in the passage in Colossians, makes the relation very specific. He says, "Here ["In this new relation" Williams; "In this new man" Phillips] there cannot be Greek and Jew, circumcised and uncircumcised, barbarian, Scythian, slave, free man, but Christ is all, and in all" (Col. 3:11). Notice how strong and positive the statement is. In this new relation, which results from the new nature, man-made differences "cannot be"; "there is no room for" them. Even the Scythians, the most barbaric of the barbarians, are included. In Christ the most radical human differences are erased. Hostile camps that divide men are abolished. If Paul were writing today to your church or mine, do you suppose he would say, "Here, or in this new relation, there cannot be Negro and white . . ."?

Let us refer back, for a moment, to Paul's emphasis on our progressive renewal in knowledge, which certainly means our progressive attainment of the image of God. By combining verses 10 and 11, and emphasizing maturing and then the elimination in Christ of man-made divisions, it would seem that Paul suggests that the Christian's ethical and spiritual maturity, his likeness to the image of God can be measured by the degree that cultural, national, and racial differences have no significance for him. Does this suggestion tend to make us a little uncomfortable? Are we still babes in Christ in our racial attitudes? Spiritual maturity on the part of God's people of all races would go a long way toward finding a solution for our present problem.

We will admit that the ideals that Paul sets out, not only in these verses from Ephesians and Colossians but elsewhere, are still a long way ahead of most modern Christians. But we would insist that "race distinctions . . . disappear in Christ and in the new man in Christ," and that he "has obliterated the words barbarian, master, slave, all of them, and has substituted the word *adelphos* (brother)."[9] This is our hope! This is our prayer!

God's Attitude Toward Man

There are many things in the Bible concerning God's attitude toward man, but of particular significance from the viewpoint of race relations and the controversy over segregation and desegregation is the fact that God's love, to use Luther's expression, is "round and whole," that he shows no partiality and is no respecter of persons.

9 *Ibid.*, IV, 503.

There is abundant evidence of this fact both in the Old Testament and in the New Testament. The Old Testament, for example, reveals that God

> shows no partiality to princes,
> nor regards the rich more than the poor,
> for they are all the work of his hands.
>
> [Job 34:19]

Judges were admonished to judge impartially (2 Chron. 19:5-7).

God is also revealed in the Old Testament as being impartial in his dealings with nations and peoples. He might bless, to an unusual degree, a people such as his chosen people, but he always did so that they might be a blessing. He plainly revealed to them that he not only used them but also other peoples to accomplish his purposes in the world. There is no justification for any nation or people to develop a messiah complex, feeling that they are the "elect of the Lord" and that he cannot do his work without them. "Judgment in history falls heaviest on those who come to think themselves gods,"[10] and not only nations but also racial and religious groups may, in a sense, consider themselves as gods.

Jesus, over and over again, revealed that he was no respecter of persons, that he showed no partiality. He was a friend of the despised publicans and sinners (Matt. 11:19), ate with them (Luke 5:29-30), and chose one of them (Levi or Matthew) as a member of the inner circle of his disciples. The Master, on at least one occasion, had some kind words even for a harlot (Luke 7:36-50). He was friendly in his attitude toward and relation to the Samaritans, with whom the Jews had no dealings. He introduced the Samaritan woman to the living water (John 4:1-42), did not even bother to reply to the charge of the Jews that he was a Samaritan (John 8:48), possibly considering the charge of no consequence, made a Samaritan the hero of one of his greatest stories (Luke 10:25-37), called attention to the fact that of the ten lepers who were healed only the Samaritan in the group

[10] Herbert Butterfield, *Christianity and History* (New York, Scribner's, 1950), p. 60.

returned to thank him (Luke 17:11–19), and included Samaria, in a special way, in the commission he gave his disciples (Acts 1:8). One cannot imagine Jesus giving any consideration to the outer conditions of men or the color of their skin. He looked on the heart.

It was Peter who stated very plainly and positively that God was no respecter of persons and showed no partiality. He made the statement in the house of Cornelius. It was the opening statement of his sermon or message or at least of the digest of his message. What Peter said was, "Now I really understand" (Goodspeed), "I see quite plainly" (Moffatt), or "I am catching on"[11] that God is no respecter of persons and shows no partiality.

Prejudiced Peter had had to have a vision on a housetop to start him in that direction. He was a typical Jew of his day, bound or restricted by many customs and taboos. God through a vision or a trance revealed to him that he must not call common or unclean anything that God had cleansed. "The meaning of the vision went far beyond the eating of food that was ceremonially unclean."

Some people argue that Peter's experience and the basic principle that he stated applied and is supposed to apply exclusively to the spiritual area. God shows no partiality in his condemnation for sin, or in the provision he makes for salvation from sin. Those are obvious truths, but how tragic for us if we consider this the total meaning of the "no-respecter-of-persons" principle.

What does the record itself reveal? Peter, when he first entered the house of Cornelius, said, "You yourselves know how unlawful it is for a Jew to associate with or to visit any one of another nation." It was immediately following this that Peter said, "But God has shown me that I should not call any man common or unclean" (Acts 10:28). The one question that some of the uncircumcision party in the church at Jerusalem asked Peter about the Cornelius experience was, "Why did you go to uncircumcised men and eat with them?" (Acts 11:3). What a contribution it would make to the solution of our present segregation-desegregation controversy if Christians, both white and Negro, both North and South, could honestly say with

11 Frank Stagg, *The Book of Acts* (Nashville, Broadman Press, 1955), p. 120.

Peter, "Now I am beginning really to catch on that God is no respecter of persons, that he shows no partiality."

There is abundant evidence in the Scriptures that the followers of Christ recognized the importance of the "no-respecter-of-persons" principle. In general it permeates the entire New Testament. We find it emphasized specifically in the writings of Peter (1 Peter 1:17) and Paul, who made it the theme of the first chapters of Romans. He stated the principle specifically (Gal. 2:6) and implied it in many places. An example of the latter is his wonderful statement in Galatians 3:28 (compared Rom. 10:12; 1 Cor. 12:13; Col. 3:11), which Williams translates as follows: "There is no room for ["Gone is the distinction between," Phillips] Jew or Greek, no room for slave or freeman, no room for male or female, for you are all one through union with Christ Jesus." Notice the words "there is no room," which is a simple statement of fact. "The point is that 'in Christ Jesus' race or national distinctions . . . do not exist, class differences . . . vanish, sex rivalry . . . disappears."[12] Robertson correctly says that this is a radical statement and that "candour compels one to confess that this goal has not yet been fully attained." That is true, although it is also true, as Alan Paton has said, that it is very difficult for a present-day Christian to think that God likes his race better than other races and even if he does it is almost impossible for him to say so aloud.

If Christians do not begin to comprehend more fully what it means to be impartial and to apply this great truth more consistently, "it is possible that future historians may declare the irony of ironies—that in the middle of the twentieth century, fight promoters and baseball managers did more for emancipating the Negro than did the churchmen."[13] Let all of us as Christians seek to eliminate from our lives all prejudice and all discrimination against any class or race. Our heavenly Father is no respecter of persons; he shows no partiality; may we increasingly be like him.

James applies the "no-respecter-of-persons" principle to the church

[12] Robertson, *op. cit.*, IV, 299.
[13] Stagg, *op. cit.*, p. 124.

in a very pointed and searching way. What he says is very definitely relevant to the segregation issue within the church itself. We shall reserve, however, a discussion of this scripture and its application to a later chapter.

Man's Relation to His Fellow Man

The Bible, in the main, contains a twofold message: how men who are lost can be saved, and how saved men are to live. There is found a twofold emphasis regarding the latter: how the saved man is to live in relation to God (the vertical) and how he is to live in relation to his fellow man and to the society of men (the horizontal). There is no question in the Bible about which of these relations comes first. Where they are found together—and they *are*, over and over again, particularly in the great summaries of the fundamental requirements of revealed religion—right relation to God is first. There is a sense in which right relation to one's fellow man derives from his right relation to God.

The Bible does reveal, however, that right relations to man inevitably result from one's right relation to God, and hence being right with one's fellow man is a proof that one is right with God. This close relationship is set out many times in the Bible. Let us call attention to only two or three instances.

Jesus taught his disciples to pray.

> And forgive us our debts,
> As we also have forgiven our
> debtors.
> [Matt. 6:12]

It may be significant that the only petition in the Model Prayer that is commented upon is this one. The statement is made: "For if you forgive men their trespasses, your heavenly Father also will forgive you; but if you do not forgive men their trespasses, neither will your Father forgive your trespasses" (Matt. 6:14–15; see Matt. 18:21–35 for a parable that illustrates the point and also reiterates the principle).

Men cannot be right with God without being right with their fellow man. This is related to and really grows out of the nature of God.

Still another illustration of the close relationship of right relations to God and to man is found in the teachings of the New Testament concerning love. When Jesus was asked for *the* great or chief commandment, he said that it was supreme love for God. Although he was not asked for a second, he, for some reason, thought it wise or necessary to add, "And a second is like it, You shall love your neighbor as yourself" (see Matt. 22:34–40).

Why did Jesus give the second when he was asked for the first or chief commandment only? There may have been several reasons, but one possible explanation was that he considered either one of the commandments incomplete without the other. No man can love God with his total personality without loving his neighbor as himself. And no man can love his neighbor as himself, with a love that partakes of the divine quality, with a love that can be described as *agape*, without loving God with his total personality. These two go together. The second is like to the first not only because it is a commandment of love but also because it is like it in importance. The two together fulfill all the requirements of God as found in the law and the prophets (cf. Rom. 13:8–10; Gal. 5:13–14; James 2:8).

The close relation of love for God and for one's fellow man is particularly central in 1 John. This little book, which is so rich in its insights into the Christian life, has as the theme for the first portion of the epistle that God is light and for the last part that God is love. The one who knows God, who has been brought into union with him, has love abiding within him. It is natural then that "he who does not love does not know God; for God is love" (1 John 4:8). John, in his typically plain-spoken way, says, "If any one says, 'I love God,' and hates his brother, he is a liar; for he who does not love his brother whom he has seen, cannot love God whom he has not seen" (1 John 4:20).

And the love John is talking about is not a mere sentimentality. It is a love that partakes of the divine quality. It is the same word that is used in John 3:16— "For God so loved the world that he gave . . ." John himself says that just as Christ laid down his life for us, which was the highest manifestation of love, "we ought to lay down our lives for the brethren" (1 John 3:16), and let us not forget that there is no color line in Christ. John also says that we are not to close or lock our hearts against a brother who is in need. If one does, he asks the searching question, "How does God's love abide in him?" (1 John 3:17). Notice that the question is "How does God's love abide in him?" rather than "How does the love of his fellow man abide in him?"

Let us repeat that our heavenly Father expects us to be like him. He is love; we show our kinship to him by loving one another. He is impartial; we are to be no respecter of persons. He manifests the fatherly attitude toward all, even those who are not in his spiritual family; we are to show the brotherly spirit toward all, even those who are not our brothers in Christ. Are we honestly striving to be like our heavenly Father? Do we see the relation of all of this to the contemporary racial situation?

A Postscript: "The Curse of Ham"

The only reason to give any space to "the curse of Ham" is the fact that so many people are using it today to justify the present racial pattern, just as their forefathers used it to defend slavery. The use of the curse stems, to a considerable degree, from the rather common tendency for men, and particularly for Christian men, to want divine approval for what they do, what they want to do, or what they think it is necessary for them to do. It seems that the more uncertain they are about the validity of their position, the more earnestly they search for something that seems to put God on their side. All of us, at times, are entirely too prone to clothe our sins in the garments of sanctity by an appeal to the Bible.

A careful study of the so-called "curse of Ham" (Gen. 9:25) will reveal that it has no significance for the present racial discussion. Let us notice first of all that the curse, pronounced by Noah, was not upon Ham but upon Canaan, one of the four sons of Ham. There is not the least suggestion in the record that it was to apply to the other three sons or to their descendants: Cush (Ethiopia), Mizraim (Egypt), and Phut or Put. The curse evidently was related to the conquest of Canaan by the children of Israel, being in a sense a prophecy that began to be fulfilled in the days of Joshua.

There is also rather general agreement that the Canaanites were not black. In speaking of the pre-Israelitish inhabitants of the Palestinian area, William F. Albright says, "All known ancient races in the region . . . belonged to the so-called 'white' or 'Caucasian' race, with the exception of the Cushites ('Ethiopians') who were strongly Negroid in type, as we know from many Egyptian paintings."[14] The Cushites were descendants of Cush, a son of Ham and a brother of Canaan.

Let us sum the matter up by citing a standard commentary on Genesis. Pieters says that even if the Negroes were of the sons of Ham, they are certainly not descendants of Canaan, and the children of Canaan were the only ones involved in the curse.[15] Even if it could be proved conclusively that the Negroes were included in the curse, would the curse still be resting upon them? Would it be perpetual? To answer in the affirmative would violate the nature of the God we find revealed in the Bible, particularly in the life and teachings of Jesus, the Son of God.

There may conceivably be social justifications for, or sociological defenses of, segregation in some areas for a period of time, but there is no valid biblical or theological defense for the segregation pattern. Some Christians may consider the present pattern necessary in their communities, but let them and all of us keep segregation as well as every other aspect of our common life under the constant judgment of the divine revelation as found in our Scriptures. Only in this way is there any hope for progress toward God's ultimate ideal for us and for our world.

[14] "The Old Testament World," *The Interpreter's Bible* (New York, Abingdon-Cokesbury Press, 1952), I, 238.
[15] *Notes on Genesis* (2d ed.; Grand Rapids, Eerdmans, 1947), p. 127.

CHAPTER SIX

Segregation and the Christian Ethic

The Christian ethic is concerned primarily with man's relation to other men and to society. There must be considerable attention given, however, to man's relation to God, since right relations to men stem from a vital relation with God. In other words, from the Christian perspective, right human relations flow from within outward. To use an old expression, there cannot be a better society without better men, and there will not be better men except as they become new creatures in Christ Jesus. The new birth gives to the individual something of God's viewpoint concerning man.

The primary source for the content of the Christian ethic is the Bible. The ethic revealed in the Bible has many dimensions. In this chapter we shall attempt to set out some of these viewpoints or dimensions. We shall also seek to show how each of them is related to the segregation-desegregation issue.

The Will of God

The Christian ethic could correctly be described as a will-of-God ethic. The will of God was central in the ethics of original Christianity. It was particularly prominent in the life and teachings of Jesus. He said repeatedly that he came not to do or to seek his own will but the will of the One who had sent him (John 5:30; 6:38). On one occasion he said to his disciples, "My food is to do the will of him who sent me, and to accomplish his work" (John 4:34). The climax of his submission to or cooperation with the will of God came in Gethsemane when he prayed, "Nevertheless, not as I will, but as thou wilt" (Matt. 26:39). Here it was, as John Bright has said, that the cross was manufactured (a word that is too mechanical) on which he was later crucified.[1]

Jesus said that entrance into the kingdom of God was and is conditioned on doing the will of God (Matt. 7:21). Kinship to him is likewise based on doing the will of his Father in heaven (Matt. 12:50). He taught his disciples to pray that the Father's will might be done on earth as it is done in heaven (Matt. 6:10). The will of God flavored all the teachings of Jesus, as was also true of Paul and other New Testament writers.

What is the significance for us of this emphasis on the will of God? It certainly means that if the will of God was so central in the life and teachings of Jesus, and in the New Testament in general, it should also be central in the Christian's life. We are not our own. We belong to God. He has the right to command. In every time of personal decision concerning any problem or any issue, the Christian should ask, "What is his will for me?" To get the answer we must ask the question sincerely; we must really want to know the will of God. Jesus himself said, "If any man's will is to do his [God's] will, he shall know whether the teaching is from God or whether I am speaking on my own authority" (John 7:17). Here is one absolutely essential requirement for a knowledge of the will of God—a willingness to do his will.

What about the application of the ethic of the will of God to the racial situation? We would agree with Everett Tilson that "what is God's will in the current racial crisis . . . is the crucial, indeed the only important, question."[2] It is with God's will that we must finally come to terms.

[1] *The Kingdom of God* (New York, Abingdon Press, 1953), p. 271.
[2] *Segregation and the Bible,* p. 116.

What about you and me: Do we really want to know God's will regarding race relations, regarding segregation and desegregation? Are we willing to do his will when we know what it is? We can be sure of this: He has a will for us, and the only way that we can have additional light concerning his will is to be true to the light that we now have.

We should also remember that in the area of race, as in every other phase of life, the will of God is the final determinant of right and wrong for those who are in the family of God. The supreme question for us is not what others think but what God thinks; not what the customs decree but what God says. The early apostles gave the classic statement of the Christian position when they said, "We must obey God rather than men" (Acts 5:29).

Turning from this brief statement concerning the individual and the will of God, let us now consider the relation of the will of God to the broader aspects of racial segregation. Let us repeat that the sovereign God of the universe, who is vitally interested in all his children, assuredly has a concern for and a will regarding the present segregation problem. To take any other position would limit the sovereignty of God. It would make of him a spectator. Such is unthinkable of the God revealed by the prophets and by Jesus.

In the light of the teachings of the Bible concerning God and his attitude toward and his relation to men, there should not be any serious question about his judgment regarding any pattern of life that would discriminate against any people because of their class, caste, or color. The God revealed in the Bible would not approve a status of subserviency for any group. Such would violate his very nature.

It may be difficult, and some would say impossible, in some sections to rise right now to the high level of the ultimate will of God in race relations. The difficulty, however, of reaching or attaining God's will does not nullify or abrogate that will. Admittedly, we have to start where we are and move toward the full achievement of his will. This is true in our individual lives. It is also true in the broader social relationships. In moving toward his will we must start where people are. This is true in the area of race relations as elsewhere. Let us be sure, however, that our movement is toward the fuller achievement of the will of God in our own lives and in the life of the world.

Does this mean an adjustment of the will of God to the realities of life? If so, would this lead us to adopt an accommodation or a compromise ethic? Is it possible that something less than the ultimate will of God might be his will for us under certain conditions?

These and similar questions pose some real problems. One thing that might be helpful would be to recognize that the expression "the will of God" may mean more than one thing. His will is so broad, so deep, so meaningful that we may need some defining terms to describe various aspects of it.

You may find helpful the distinctions made by Leslie Weatherhead between the intentional, the circumstantial, and the ultimate will of God.[3] The ultimate will of God refers to his sovereign will that finally will be done. No man nor group of men, no nation nor combination of nations can defeat God in his ultimate purposes. The last word will be his. He may lose some battles, but he never loses a war.

It seems that a valid distinction may be made between the intentional will of God, or what others have called the perfect or the directive will of God, and the circumstantial or the permissive will of God. The implication is that under certain circumstances God might approve something that is less than his intentional or perfect will. We say this "might" be true. We are inclined to believe that it is true, but we cannot speak for God.

The whole idea of the circumstantial will of God is closely akin to the "lesser-of-two-evils" theory, which is rather popular in contemporary Christian thought. Those who hold to this theory say that, since we are evil and the world in which we live is evil, many of our choices will not be between an unmixed good and an unmixed evil. Many decisions will have to be in the gray area. Some evil and some good will be involved in all such decisions.

Those who would use the "lesser-of-two-evils" theory to defend segregation should be careful how they use it. They should remember

[3] *The Will of God* (New York, Abingdon-Cokesbury, 1944).

that if a child of God chooses what he considers to be the lesser of two evils, he should always do so in the full light of God's intentional will and should always give primary consideration to the effect of his decision on the cause of Christ. In other words, the decision should be made that would contribute the maximum to the promotion of, and the minimum of damage to, the kingdom of God. As Brunner says, "The will of God is the will of God for the kingdom."[4] This entire viewpoint, if consistently maintained, will keep our accommodations, if any, in proper focus and under the constant judgment of God.

If we utilize the "lesser-of-two-evils" theory, let us not forget that our decision is the lesser of two *evils*. If we recognize clearly that there is evil involved in our decision, that it falls short of the intentional or perfect will of God, then there will remain hope for progress toward the fuller achievement of the will of God. It is this contrast between our present level of living and God's high demand on us that creates for serious-minded Christians the wholesome constructive tension which is so essential for progress in spiritual maturity.

On the other hand, striving to move as far and as rapidly as possible toward God's will for us is one essential step in the release of that tension. "The will of God is the only basis of our peace." Thoughtful Christians cannot have peace unless they are honestly attempting to know more fully and to do more perfectly the will of God in every area of their lives. This means that there must be movement toward the intentional will of God for release to come from the tension that results from a consciousness of falling short of his will. We cannot have inner satisfaction as children of God if we identify what may seem to be his circumstantial will with his intentional will and par-ticularly with his ultimate will.

Assuming that there is validity in the idea of the circumstantial or the permissive will of God for our lives, that circumstantial will is under the constant judgment of God's intentional will. And we can be sure that God would not approve, even as his circumstantial will, any action that would not contribute to the movement of our lives

4 Emil Brunner, *The Divine Imperative*, trans. Olive Wyon (Philadelphia, Westminster Press, 1953), p. 56.

and the life of the world toward his intentional will for us and his ultimate will for the world.

There is at least one other thing that should be said concerning segregation and the will of God. A man conceivably might defend segregation, under certain circumstances, and not do any great damage to the Christian ethic and to the Christian cause. He does irreparable harm, however, to both when he identifies segregation with the intentional or with the ultimate will of God. Such identification violates the very nature of the God who created man in his own image, and who has never been and is not a respecter of persons. Let us not claim the authority of God for that which is so contrary to his nature and to his revealed will.

Perfection

The Christian ethic could also be described as a perfectionistic ethic. This has been implied in what has been said concerning the ultimate and the intentional will of God. God's intentional will is his ideal, his absolute, his perfect will as contrasted to what may be his relative or permissive will. Nothing less than perfection should ever be identified with God's intentional will.

Jesus, in some very specific ways, gave emphasis to this idea of perfection. His ideal for his followers was and is that they be perfect as their Father in heaven is perfect (Matt. 5:48). The portion of this statement that gives to it its real depth and challenge is "as your Father in heaven." We may say that the word "perfect" is not the best translation. What differences does that make as long as those words "as your Father in heaven" are in there? Christ's ideal for us is that we should be like our heavenly Father. Who among us would dare to say that he even begins to approximate that ideal or standard?

Furthermore, every basic teaching of Jesus was a demand for perfection. He never gave or recognized any limits to his fundamental teachings. They were all absolute. For example, when Peter asked Jesus if he should forgive one who had sinned against him "as many as seven times," which was more generous than the Jewish requirement, the reply of Jesus was, "I do not say to you seven times, but seventy times seven" (Matt. 18:22). Jesus here said to Peter and to the other disciples, as he would say to us, that there are to be no limits to forgiveness.

Similarly, Jesus did not and would not limit the application of his teachings concerning love. He pointedly said to his disciples that they were not only to love their neighbors but also their enemies. They were to pray for those who persecuted them (Matt. 5:43-44).

When the scribe asked Jesus to define "neighbor" for him and hence to build some limiting fences for love, Jesus refused. He told the scribe the story of the Good Samaritan, and then pressed home an infinitely more important question than the one the scribe had asked. The question of Jesus was, "Which of these three, do you think, proved neighbor to the man who fell among robbers?" (Luke 10:36).

What was true of forgiveness and love was also true of the other basic teachings of Jesus. They were a part of his demands for or his ethic of perfection. His expectations were and are so high, so far beyond the reach of the natural man, that if he had said nothing about the necessity of the new birth the high call of his teachings would have assumed and necessitated it.

Jesus not only challenged the individual to be perfect; he also set out an ideal of perfection for the world. He taught his disciples to pray,

> Thy kingdom come,
> Thy will be done,
> On earth as it is in heaven.
>
> [Matt. 6:10]

If God's will were done on earth as it is in heaven it would be done perfectly. If it were done perfectly, then his kingdom would come completely. To this end we are to pray and work.

We must admit again that none of us lives up fully to these high demands of Jesus. None of us is perfect. The society in which we live is far from perfect. Can the Lord expect us to apply the concept of perfection to our contemporary situation? What would his perfect demands mean in the area of race relations? Is it possible for us to apply those ideas and ideals in our immediate situation? We have sought before to answer these questions, at least to some degree, under our discussion of the will of God. We said there that his intentional will is his perfect will. We have also suggested that there may be such a thing as his circumstantial will, but that his circumstantial will would always keep us moving in the direction of his intentional will, would always contribute, to some degree, to the attainment of his ultimate will.

In the light of these distinctions what, if any, relevance does the idea or ethic of perfection have for us in our day? Will it provide any practical source of guidance for us as we seek to determine what should be the Christian's position regarding segregation and other contemporary issues?

While we may not derive as much immediate help as we should like from the ideals of perfection, yet it is possible that those ideals which we find so prevalent in our Bible, and particularly in the teachings of Jesus, are the most abidingly relevant portions of the Bible. Ideals that could be attained or reached in a day, a month, a year, or even in a lifetime would be limited in their relevance. Once reached they would lose their challenge.

The ideals of perfection, on the other hand, are constantly before us, to use a term of Reinhold Niebuhr's, as "impossible possibilities." They are theoretically possible, while we know that we shall never fully reach them. It is this seeming paradox that makes them abidingly challenging and hence forever relevant.

This also means that we can never equate any human achievement in our lives or in the world with the kingdom of God, with God's full and final will. The kingdom is in the world but not of the world. It is a dynamic force in the world, but it cannot be realized by or contained in any human or worldly program. It is God who finally gives us the kingdom.

One reason for the continuing relevance of the ideal of perfection is the fact that it is a progressive ideal. God expects his children to move toward perfection; but rather paradoxically as we move toward what we consider to be perfection our insights into its meaning are deepened and the ideal moves ahead of us. This is the experience of a maturing child of God, of any one who is continuously led by or walks under the guiding impulse of the Spirit of God.

We should be eternally grateful, however, that God does not judge us by whether or not we are perfect. He does judge us by the direction of our lives. His question is not so much, "Are you perfect?" but rather, "Are you moving toward perfection?" He may also ask a companion question, "How rapidly are you moving in that direction?" What would our answers have to be? Do we have an uneasy conscience at this point?

There can certainly be no question about what a perfect society would be racially. There would be no compulsory segregation with its inevitable discrimination. There would be no second-class citizens in a "first-class" society. Our society is far from that ideal. Is it moving in that direction? If not, the judgment of God rests upon it.

Love

The Christian ethic is frequently labeled an ethic of love, or more fully of "obedient love,"[5] "cross-embracing love,"[6] or "the radical ethic of love."[7]

The radical and the sacrificial cross-bearing elements are inherent, to a considerable degree, in the rather characteristic word for love, which is used so frequently in the New Testament. This word *agape*, in its various forms, is so distinctive that some New Testament scholars believe it should have been transliterated rather than translated.

There are several relatively unique qualities about *agape* as compared to other types or forms of love. One thing frequently revealed in the New Testament is that *agape* gives itself to the object loved. Its language is the language of self-sacrifice, of self-denial, of cross

[5] See Paul Ramsey, *Basic Christian Ethics* (New York, Scribner's, 1950).
[6] Toyohiko Kagawa, *Brotherhood Economics* (New York, Harper, 1936), p. 34.
[7] John Bennett, *et al.*, *Christian Values and Economic Life* (New York, Harper, 1954), p. 206.

bearing. We see this in such statements as: "For God so loved the world that he gave . . ." (John 3:16); "Christ loved the church and gave himself up for her" (Eph. 5:25); "The Son of God . . . loved me and gave himself for me" (Gal. 2:20); and, "Greater love has no man than this, that a man lay down his life for his friends" (John 15:13).

To the disciples Jesus said, "This is my commandment, that you love one another as I have loved you" (John 15:12). Did he mean as much as he had loved them? If so, he loved them enough to give his life for them; they should love enough to give their lives for one another. He had previously said to them, "If you love me, you will keep my commandments" (John 14:15; cf. 14:21, 24). One test of our love for him is our willingness to keep his commandments and one very specific commandment is that we love one another, and "one another" includes all who are his disciples.

The so-called Golden Rule, which is a practical expression of love, is very definitely and disturbingly relevant to the racial situation. In Luke's gospel, where it is specifically related to love, it is stated as follows: "And as you wish that men would do to you, do so to them" (Luke 6:31). Williams, bringing out the verb tense as he typically does, translates the parallel verse in Matthew as follows: "You must practice dealing with others as you would like for them to deal with you" (Matt. 7:12).

What if the white people were in the minority? What if we were the ones who were segregated? What would we want the controlling majority to do to and for us? Would not the application of the Golden Rule go a long way toward solving the segregation problem for us and for our society?

An emphasis on love is very prevalent in the epistles of Paul. He said that love fulfilled the requirements of the law ("is the perfect satisfaction of the law" Williams). One reason for this was and is the fact that "love does no wrong to a neighbor" ("love hurts nobody" Phillips) (Rom. 13:10). Do we need to say again that "neighbor" as used in the Bible and as defined from the Christian perspective knows no color line?

Paul admonished the Ephesians, "Walk in love" (Eph. 5:2). The significance of this admonition is greatly heightened when we see what is immediately before and after it. Notice the full quotation of verses 1 and 2: "Therefore be imitators of God ["keep on following God's example," Williams], as beloved children. And walk in love ["practice living in love," Williams], as Christ loved us and gave himself up for us, a fragrant offering and sacrifice to God."

Paul, in writing to the Colossians, said that those who had been raised with Christ should not only put off all things contrary to the new life in Christ but that they should also put on or clothe themselves with the qualities of the new life in Christ, such as compassion, kindness, patience, and the other positive qualities of Christian living. He then added that "above all these" or "over all these qualities" (Williams) they should put on love "which binds everything together in perfect harmony" (Col. 3:14). Lightfoot suggests that love is the outer garment or the girdle that holds the others in their places.

The primacy of love is found elsewhere in Paul's epistles. To the Thessalonians he wrote, "And may the Lord make you increase and abound ["overflow" Williams] in love to one another and to all men ..." (1 Thess. 3:12). Notice here the all-inclusiveness of "to all men." In the great passage on the fruit of the Spirit, the first fruit Paul mentions is love, which might suggest that it is the source of the others and that which gives unity to all (Gal. 5:22; cf. 2 Peter 1:7, where love is the highest step in a stair-step type of outline of Christian virtues).

Paul, after setting out the gifts of the Spirit, in 1 Corinthians 12, introduces his great love chapter with the statement, "I will show you a still more excellent way," "the highest way of all" (Phillips), "a way that is better by far" (Williams), " 'a way *par excellence*,' beyond all comparison" (A. T. Robertson). It is this love or *agape* that is the "more excellent way" in race relations and in human relations in general. Legislation and court actions may be and are necessary, but love is "a way that is better by far." Educational programs and political action may be and will be necessary, but Christian love is "the highest way of all." Love (*agape*) must infuse and inform all the efforts to solve the race problem, if those efforts are to be most effective.

Paul ends this great passage on love by saying, "So faith, hope, love abide, these three; but the greatest of these is love." He then adds an admonition that applies as definitely to us as to the Corinthians. It is, "Make love your aim" ("keep on pursuing love," Williams). The Corinthians, torn by divisions and strife, had not fully attained love; they needed to make it their aim or keep on pursuing it. That was not only true of them; it is also true of us. We should persistently follow after love, knowing that we shall never completely comprehend its height, its depth, its breadth.

Let us permit a few of the central verses of 1 Corinthians 13 to search our hearts. Paul outlines some of the characteristics of love as follows:

Love is patient and kind; love is not jealous or boastful; it is not arrogant or rude. Love does not insist on its own way; it is not irritable or resentful; it does not rejoice at wrong, but rejoices in the right. Love bears all things, believes all things, hopes all things, endures all things.
Love never ends [fails].

[I Cor. 13:4–8]

The love that never fails or "survives everything" is *agape*. It is a love that possesses the divine qualities Paul enumerates. We do not possess them fully, but are we making them our aim, are we pursuing them, are we making progress in the attainment of them? If we are, then our relations with others in the home, in the church, and in the community will be constantly improving.

The emphasis on love and on the ethic of love was not only prominent in the life and teachings of Jesus and in the writings of Paul but also in the writings of John. We shall restrict our consideration to 1 John, seeking to avoid any duplication of what has been said previously concerning the epistle.

The author states as one purpose of the epistle that those who read it might know that they had eternal life (5:13). He presents three main proofs that one has eternal life as a present possession. They are one's relation to Christ, to sin, and to his brothers in Christ. The test of right relation to the brethren is love for them. John makes this emphasis over and over again. For example, he says, "We know that we have passed out of (migrated from) death into life, because we love the brethren" (3:14); "He who loves his brother abides in the light" (2:10); and again he says, "Every one who loves the parent [God] loves the child [the one born of God]" (5:1).

Let us repeat that one of the proofs to ourselves and to others that we have eternal life in quality as well as eternal in time is the quality of the life we live. One important element in life with the eternal quality is that we reveal the attitudes and maintain the relations that would be in harmony with and reflect credit to the Eternal Person, who is love, and who, living within us, gives to us eternal life. "He who has the Son has life; he who has not the Son has not life" (5:12). The Eternal One within us is not only the source of life, but also of the light that will drive out the darkness of sin, and of the love that will reach out in a spirit of active good will to all men —to non-Christians as well as Christians, to enemies as well as friends. If the love, *agape*, of Christ controls us, we will know no partiality, no essential differences, no feelings of superiority or inferiority.

The Cross

The Christian ethic is basically an ethic of the cross. It seems, however, that comparatively few Christians think of the cross as having any particular relevance for the everyday problems of life. They think of the cross almost exclusively in terms of Calvary. We do not mean to deprecate that cross in any measure. It is the central event, along with the empty tomb, of both human and divine history. That cross was a very real one on which Christ, Son of Man and Son of God, gave his life to redeem mankind from the final penalty and from the present power of sin. Rightly we sing of that cross; but unfortunately we sing of it as the old rugged cross "on a hill far away." The expression "on a hill far away" reveals rather accurately our attitude toward the cross.

Some of us may recognize that the cross not only awaited Jesus at the end of his earthly journey, but also that it filled an important place in his life. While he walked among men we may understand, at least to a limited degree, that he walked under the constant and deepening shadow of the cross. We may comprehend that the cross on which he died was accepted in the Garden. We may believe, although we cannot fully understand, that his death on Calvary was a natural, a more or less inevitable climax of the kind of life he had lived; that his death was really a continuation of his life.

Even if we have that much insight into the meaning of the cross, we must confess that few of us want any part of the cross for ourselves. "We are possessed of the notion that the Cross is for Christ, a once-and-for-all thing of the past tense."[8] The cross, when properly understood, is not exclusively for Christ. Neither is it a once-and-for-all thing of the past tense. Jesus is not supposed to bear the cross alone and all the world go free. "No, there's a cross for every one, and there's a cross for me." There must be if we are to follow Christ.

It was at Caesarea Philippi, after Peter had given the great confession for himself and for the other disciples, that Jesus began to reveal more fully to them that he was to go to Jerusalem and be crucified. It was immediately following this revelation that he said to them and to all the multitude, "If any man would come after me, let him deny himself and take up his cross and follow me" (Matt. 16:24; cf. Mark 8:34 and Luke 9:23).

Taking up a cross or denying self is voluntary. Jesus will never force a cross on any man. Yet, taking up a cross is necessary if we are to follow him. As Bonhoeffer, a modern Christian martyr, has said, the suffering it represents "is an essential part of the specifically Christian life."[9] Since the Master's demands are always absolute, and since none of us measures up fully, we can correctly say that to the degree we take up a cross, to the degree we deny ourselves, to that degree and to that degree only do we really follow Christ. We should understand that suffering which can be identified with the cross is suffering for the sake of Christ and his cause. Its purpose and ultimate end is redemptive.

[8] Bright, *op. cit.*, p. 269.
[9] *The Cost of Discipleship* (New York, Macmillan, 1948), p. 72.

A cross is something on which one dies. In the spiritual sense it involves the crucifixion of the self, with selfish ambitions and purposes. It was Paul who said, "I have been crucified with Christ; it is no longer I who live, but Christ who lives in me" (Gal. 2:20; cf. Gal. 5:24; 6:14; Rom. 6:6, 8). This comes as near to a definition of the meaning of the cross for the Christian as anything we find in the Scriptures. Paul had been crucified with Christ at the time of his conversion, when he was brought into union with Christ. Yet, his crucifixion was evidently a continuing experience. Paul could go so far as to say, "For to me to live is Christ" (Phil. 1:21), or, "Living is coextensive with Christ."

Paul's whole ethical emphasis, which incidentally is very important in his epistles, makes quite central the element of self-denial, symbolized by the cross. He stresses repeatedly that the liberty the Christian has in Christ is to be surrendered voluntarily for the sake of Christ and also for the sake of others. When one is brought into a vital life-changing union with Christ, he becomes a new creation in Christ Jesus. He is freed from the condemnation of the law, from the enslavement of sin, and ultimately from the destructive separation of death. He is a free man, but he becomes a slave of Christ. Really, only as he becomes a slave of Christ and righteousness can he know fully freedom from sin and Satan (see Rom. 6).

Throughout his epistles Paul seemed to fear that some children of God would abuse the freedom they had in Christ. This fear provides the background for his statement of a basic position, as clearly set out in the Galatian letter as anywhere. To the Galatians he wrote: "For you, brothers, were called to freedom; only you must not let your freedom be an excuse for the gratification of your lower nature, but in love be slaves to one another" (Gal. 5:13, Williams). He then ties this statement in with love of neighbor. If we, in our day, love God supremely and love our neighbor as ourselves we shall voluntarily surrender our freedom, if need be, for the sake of God's kingdom and for the good of our neighbor.

Paul, near the close of his lengthy discussion of the eating of meat offered to idols, which provides a very practical and comparatively simple application of the ethic of self-denial, sums up the matter as follows: "Let no one seek his own good, but the good of his neighbor" (1 Cor. 10:24). This would solve the problem for the Corinthians of eating meat offered to idols. If accepted and followed consistently, it would also answer many of our questions about daily conduct and would contribute a great deal to the solution of our most perplexing social and moral problems, including the problem of segregation and desegregation.

This voluntary self-denial, with a redemptive purpose or goal, which can properly be called an ethic of the cross, is abidingly pertinent for our world and its problems. The cross is God's strategy for overcoming sin not only in the individual's life but also in the life of the world. What does this mean in the area of race relations? Does it mean that those who belong to the oppressed minority are to bear patiently any injustice and discrimination? Is this their cross? This could be a cross in the Christian sense only if it was accepted voluntarily and was redemptive in its outcome.

The cross applies in a particular way to the majority, to the powerful, to the privileged. They are the ones who can voluntarily correct the evils and ills of our society. They are the ones to whom the voluntary principle will apply in a particular way. The cross for them can mean the denial of self, the sacrifice of privilege for the sake not only of others but also for the sake of society, and what is more important, for the sake of the cause of Christ.

Changes in patterns of life are brought about, in the main, in one of two ways: by pressure and the use of force or by peaceful methods. The latter is the Christian method for change. The only hope for a peaceful solution, with a minimum even of social pressure, for the contemporary racial crisis is that the powerful and privileged majority will accept the responsibility to find a solution in harmony with the Christian spirit and Christian teachings.

Let us sum up by saying that the cross, and what it symbolizes, is the central distinctive unifying element in original Christian ethics. We must, in the contemporary period, return to this central emphasis and understand more clearly what the cross means in the

Christian's life if we are to revitalize organized Christianity and to make the Christian ethic a dynamic factor in meeting the world's needs. "The way of the cross leads home" for the individual; it is the way for his redemption. The cross also is the way of social reconstruction and moral reformation.

The Holy Spirit

The Holy Spirit, as a member of the godhead, is revealed in the Bible as a moral being, possessing the same qualities of moral personality as God the Father. The ethic found in the Bible is an ethic of the Holy Spirit. It is this fact that sets the Christian ethic most sharply apart from all other ethical systems.

We need, in our day, to rediscover the work of the Spirit, particularly in the area of everyday Christian living. He has a number of functions he would perform for us and contributions he would make to us if we would let him.

One of the main works of the Spirit is to convict of sin. This he does not only for the non-Christian but also for the Christian. All of us, Christians as well as non-Christians, have gone astray; we have come short of the glory of God; we have sinned; there is none that is righteous, no, not one. We all need to repent of our sins and ask God to forgive us. For the non-Christian this will result in the new birth, which is the basic hope for personal ethical living and for social and moral advance. For the Christian, repentance will lead to restoration of fellowship with God and to a deepened insight into the nature and will of God for one's life and for the life of the world.

Are we, as Christians, willing to ask the Spirit of God to show us our sins in the area of race relations? If we are, the vast majority of us will become conscious that we have sinned, that we have fallen short of God's expectation for us, that we have missed the mark he has set for us in this area of our lives. This will be true of Negro and white, of desegregationist and segregationist. There is none of us righteous enough to feel self-righteous. We will see this clearly if our spirits have been touched by the Holy Spirit. Will we, all of us, repent of our sins against our neighbors of other races and ask God to give us the strength to live as we should for him?

Another aspect of the work of the Holy Spirit is that he is to lead the child of God in his search for and insight into the truth of God. Jesus suggested this when he said, "When the Spirit of truth comes, he will guide you into all the truth" (John 16:13). This does not necessarily mean that he would lead to the discovery of new truth, truth not previously revealed by Jesus. It seems to mean, primarily, that the Spirit would lead them to discover the truth there was in Christ. And who would dare to say, even in our day, that he has exhausted the truth revealed by and in Christ?

Paul says that the Spirit searches even the depths of God (1 Cor. 2:10). The Holy Spirit fully comprehends the nature, the grace, the will and purpose of God. "No one comprehends the thoughts of God except the Spirit of God" (1 Cor. 2:11). If we want to know the mind and will of God, let us learn from and be taught by the Spirit, whose function it is to interpret "spiritual truths to those who possess the Spirit" (1 Cor. 2:13). If we want to know what is God's will for us in the area of race relations, let us learn of the Spirit. He will lead us into a fuller knowledge of the truth if we will let him. Also, under the impact of the divine Spirit the truth that we find in the Scriptures will become vital and alive. It will become for us the living Word, as under the Spirit's leadership we respond to its appeal.

The Christian's ethical life is matured in the Spirit. In other words, as we increasingly walk in or under the guiding impulse of the Spirit we mature as children of God. We become more sensitive to sin in our lives. We will have increasingly the victory over the sins of the flesh (Gal. 5:16 ASV), but at the same time we will become more conscious of the sins of the spirit. Walking under the guiding impulse of the Spirit, we shall become more mature in our judgment of what is right and wrong.

The Spirit not only will guide us to see more clearly the difference between right and wrong; he will also give us, as we respond to him, the power to overcome sin, to resist the wrong and to do the right. This power is one of the greatest needs in our lives. Without the energizing of the Spirit effective Christian living is impossible, the Christian ethic is impractical.

The Spirit is the source of the wonderful fruit that Paul speaks of in the Galatian letter: "Love, joy, peace, patience, kindness, goodness, faithfulness, gentleness, self-control" (Gal. 5:22–23). This list of fruit might be considered as God's standard of excellence. How do we measure up when we lay our lives down beside this standard? How much is there in our lives of the fruit of the Spirit? What would our neighbors say? What would our acquaintances of other races say? What does our own better self say?

Notice that these are the fruit (singular) of the Spirit. This suggests unity as contrasted to the works (plural) of the flesh. It is also true that fruit is normal, natural, and inevitable. Some evidence of the fruit of the Spirit will be in our lives if the Spirit dwells within us. The degree or yield of the fruit will be determined by how obediently and consistently we walk under the guiding impulse of the Spirit.

The naturalness of the fruit also suggests its inwardness. Some of the qualities mentioned—love, joy, and peace—are definitely inner. The other qualities, or fruit, are the natural expression of what is on the inside. The movement in the Christian life is from the inside to the outside. This is the reason why the Christian religion and the Christian ethic are primarily concerned with Christian character rather than with Christian conduct. The latter will result from the former. The only sound, dependable basis for Christian conduct is in Christian character, which stems from union with Christ.

There is at least one other work or function of the Spirit that should be mentioned. It has tremendous implications for race relations. The matter has been mentioned before and will be discussed briefly again in the next chapter. Where the Spirit operates there is created not only unity within the individual Christian but also among Christians. The Spirit creates a fellowship, a *koinonia*. He did it at Pentecost when he came in power. The record says that "the company of those who believed were of one heart and soul" (Acts 4:32). This spirit of unity and fellowship went so deep that they sold what they had and shared with those in need.

Since Pentecost the Holy Spirit has been active in breaking down barriers that divide people. His presence and power were seen in the vision of Peter on the housetop and in Peter's visit to the house of Cornelius. It was the Holy Spirit that led Peter to see that he was not to call any man common or unclean. It was the Spirit that enabled him to say, "Truly, I perceive that God shows no partiality."

Schools and churches may be desegregated without the achievement of unity or genuine fellowship. Desegregation might even contribute to disunity and to the destruction of fellowship. The only way to attain real integration, if by "integration" we mean the acceptance of those of various races into full fellowship with all the rights and privileges of that fellowship, is in the work of the Holy Spirit.

On the other hand, if the Holy Spirit lives in us and possesses us, we shall contribute what we can to the unity and fellowship of all who know him. Let us remember that "by one Spirit we were all baptized into one body—Jews or Greeks, slaves or free—and all were made to drink of one Spirit" (1 Cor. 12:13). We agree with Henlee Barnette that "racial differences are wholly disregarded by the Holy Spirit," that "He knows no racial distinction." One evidence of this is that he "continues to descend upon people of all races." How could it be otherwise, when God is no respecter of persons?

Whether we think of the Christian ethic as primarily an ethic of the will of God, of perfection, of obedient or self-sacrificing love, of the cross, or of the Holy Spirit, we will find a challenge in it in our relations to peoples of other classes and races. The challenge may seem to be far beyond our ability to attain. We may even consider the whole Christian ethic approach to the racial situation to be not only very idealistic but also irrelevant and impractical.

We admit, as we have formerly, that the high demands of the Christian ethic are far beyond our present level of living and even beyond general attainment in the foreseeable future. We insist, however, that this fact does not make the Christian ethic either irrelevant or impractical. Its basic ideas and ideals are abidingly relevant. They give us goals to strive for to the end of life's journey. They continually stand in judgment against us not only for our very imperfect way of living but also for our unwillingness to face or hear "the upward call of God in Christ Jesus" (Phil. 3:14). It may be that God condemns us more for our unwillingness to accept and to measure our lives by his standards than for our inability to attain to them.

CHAPTER SEVEN

The Church and Segregation

In this chapter we shall take a frank look at the church. We shall ask, in a more specific way than formerly, what the church should do about segregation within its own ranks. In seeking an answer we shall examine the nature of the church and the relation of its nature to racial exclusiveness or inclusiveness. After this has been done, we shall appraise the achievement of the churches in the area of racial desegregation and set forth some of the problems the churches face in implementing in the area of race relations the ideals they preach and teach.

The word "church" is used in so many different ways that it may be wise to make a brief statement concerning its use in this chapter. Sometimes "church" is used to refer to the church universal composed of all the redeemed. When so used, it is usually capitalized—the Church. Frequently, it is used to refer to a local congregation. There are still others who write or speak from a rather general perspective, who use "the church" in an institutional sense. They make it parallel to similar terms, such as "the home," "the school," and "the state." They suggest that each of these expressions stands for or symbolizes fairly well defined and relatively distinctive functions of the social order. The term "the church" will be used in this chapter, to some degree, with all of these meanings. It is believed that the particular meaning will always be fairly clear.

We shall look first, however, at the nature of the church as revealed by a study of the New Testament. This will reveal the divine ideal for the church. Only those aspects of the nature of the church will be considered that are particularly pertinent for race relations.

"The Church of God"

Paul, in an expression found only in his epistles, refers a number of times to "the church of God," and in one place to "the church of the living God" (1 Tim. 3:15). He also speaks of "the churches of God" (1 Thess. 2:14; 1 Cor. 11:16). An examination will be made of only two passages, both of which are found in 1 Corinthians. These passages are considered particularly appropriate for this study of segregation and desegregation.

A report had been brought to Paul that divisions had arisen in the Corinthian church. The fact of these divisions may give added weight or significance to Paul's use of "the church of God" in his salutation in both 1 Corinthians and 2 Corinthians.

What does Paul mean when he addresses the Corinthian Christians as "the church of God which is at Corinth" (1 Cor. 1:2)? It may be that by "the church" he merely meant "the people of God," "God's congregation," or "God's group of called-out ones." They had been called, as Paul specifically suggests, to be saints, to be sanctified, consecrated, or dedicated by or through their union with Christ Jesus. Paul further suggests that they shared this call "with all those who in every place call on the name of our Lord Jesus Christ." Here is a broad fellowship that extends beyond the local group at Corinth. It extends to those of other classes and races. It is a shared fellowship through union with and in Christ.

Those who have been brought into a living union with Christ are a "divinely gathered people," assembled or called out by God but also called before him or to be in his presence and called to live for him. They and the church they compose, whether at Corinth or anywhere else, belong to God and not to any man, group of men, or faction. The church at Corinth was the church of God. It was not Peter's church, Apollos' church, or even Paul's church. It did not belong to any one or all of the parties that had usurped the name of those great Christian leaders.

There is another place in 1 Corinthians (10:32) where Paul uses the expression "the church of God,"[1] which has real importance for race relations. The context of the verse gives to it added significance. Let us look briefly at that context. Paul was near the conclusion of his rather lengthy discussion of the Christian's voluntary surrender of his freedom, which he had illustrated with the case of the eating of meat offered to idols. He sums up the entire matter by saying, "Whether you eat or drink, or whatever you do, do all to the glory of God" (v. 31). This "embraces all of life." Notice the end or goal of a Christian's conduct: "to the glory of God." This should be the ruling motive in the life of the child of God. To reveal God and hence to glorify him also means that one will not give offense, be an occasion of stumbling, or trip Jews or Greeks or "the church of God" (v. 32). Here is an all-inclusive exhortation.

Christians will glorify God and will "give no offense" to the church or to those who are outside the Christian fellowship, if they will honestly and sincerely seek to reveal to the world the nature, the character, and the will of the God who is their Father and also the Father of all who believe. Let us ask ourselves: Do we really seek to glorify God in our attitudes toward and relations to those of other races?

Paul would say to us as he did to the Corinthians: "Be imitators of me, as I am of Christ" (1 Cor. 11:1) ("Follow my example just as I myself am following Christ's," Williams). He said that he did not seek his own advantage: Do we? He said that he sought to please all men: Do we? He gave as the motive that others might be saved: Is that the motive in our lives?

"The Body of Christ"

This is another term or expression used by Paul to refer to the church. For him the church was not only "the church of God" but also "the body of Christ." He applied the analogy of the body rather

---

[1] For additional references see 1 Cor. 11:22; 15:9; 2 Cor. 1:1; Gal. 1:22; and 1 Tim. 3:5.

frequently and thoroughly to the church. The fullest development of this idea is found in 1 Corinthians and in Ephesians. The passage from 1 Corinthians (12:12–31), as was true of the other passages that we have used from this letter, has added import because of the problems that had arisen in Corinth. There were dissensions in the church at Corinth; there is no dissension in the body with its different members and should not be in the church which Paul calls the body of Christ. There are different functions for the various members of the body to perform, but each function is essential and important. That is true of the human body. It is also true of the spiritual body—the church. It is in the Roman letter that Paul similarly says, "For as in one body we have many members, and all the members do not have the same function, so we, though many, are one body in Christ, and individually members one of another" (Rom. 12:4–5).

The various gifts or functions are for a common purpose: "For the equipment of the saints, . . . for building up the body of Christ, until we all attain to the unity of the faith . . . to mature manhood, to the measure of the stature of the fullness of Christ ["to a mature manhood and to a perfect measure of Christ's moral stature," Williams]: . . . into him who is the head, into Christ" (Eph. 4:12–15). God has so perfectly adjusted the members or parts of the body to one another "that there is no disharmony in the body" (Williams).

What God has done for the body, he wants to do and will do, if his children will let him, for his church. If we will let him there will be such a sense of oneness in the spiritual body, the church, that if one member suffers, all will suffer together; if one member is honored, all will rejoice with him (1 Cor. 12:26).

The introductory verses of the great section in 1 Corinthians on the church as the body of Christ are of special importance for our study. Phillips translates these verses as follows:

As the human body, which has many parts, is a unity, and those parts, despite their multiplicity, comprise together one single body, so it is with the Body of Christ. For we were all baptized by the Spirit into one Body, whether we were Jews, Gentiles, slaves or free men, and we have all had experience of the same Spirit ["were all imbued with one Spirit," Williams].

Christians should never forget that those of every class, color, and condition of life who have been brought into a life-changing union with Christ are members of the body of Christ. They have been "imbued" by the same Spirit. It is this union with Christ, this enduement of the Spirit, that gives to them their unity even in their diversity. There may be and are many members with varying abilities and functions, but they are one body.

Another thing that gives unity to the body of Christ is the fact that Christ is the head of the body, which is his church (Eph. 5:23; Col. 1:18). This is just as true of the local congregation as it is of the general body of the redeemed.

Christ is described in the Bible not only as the head of the church but also of every man (1 Cor. 11:3), "of all rule and authority" (Col. 2:10), and of "all things" (Eph. 1:22). The expression in Ephesians is of particular interest. Paul says in verses 22 and 23 that "he [God] has put all things under his feet and has made him the head over all things for ["to" ASV] the church, which is his body, the fulness of him who fills all in all."

If the "for" is correct, then the purpose of Christ's headship over all is for the good of the church. This would certainly greatly magnify the church, the people of God. On the other hand, if "to" is correct, then it means that the one who has been given to be head of the church is the same One who has been made head over all things. This means that the head of the church is the highly exalted One, "above all rule and authority," "above every name that is named." These facts do not only magnify his authority over the church but also highly honor the church itself. Its head is the One who is head over all things, the One, as Paul says in Philippians, to whom every knee will bow and every tongue will confess (Phil. 2:10–11). How willingly and joyfully should the church and the members of Christ's body follow and be obedient to such a head and leader!

Christ's sovereignty over all other areas of life may be for the sake of his church. But his sovereignty over and in his church is for the glory of God. The church, if it is to glorify God, must cooperate with him in extending his authority and control over every area of life. He cannot be Lord or sovereign at all unless he is sovereign over all.

This means that the church, in a very true sense, looks in two directions at the same time. It looks toward its sovereign Head from whom it gets its orders or directions. On the other hand, it looks toward the world, where it is to extend his sovereignty by carrying out his orders. No organization called a church is really a church of God unless it has this two-way look. However, the look toward the world must be through the eyes of the One who is the head of the church, and who has the authority to command. This One knows no east or west, north or south, Jew or Gentile, red or yellow, black or white.

Let us consider briefly what it would mean if churches took seriously the fact that they are "churches of God," that they are "the body of Christ." They would first of all realize that a church is not a fraternal order, a civic club, or a business concern. Although it is composed of very real men and women, boys and girls, it is a unique institution with a distinctive function to perform. It is God's institutional mediator between himself and the world. It is in the world as his representative. One of its chief functions is to make men and the community of men conscious of the presence of the living God. Its spire points symbolically upward toward God. The members are so to live among men that they will point them to God.

This means that the churches should maintain high standards for church membership. They not only have a right but a responsibility to determine the requirements for membership in them. In most cases those requirements for admittance and standards for the continuance of membership should be higher than they are. However, all such requirements or standards should be brought under the scrutiny of the Head of the church. They should be standards that would glorify God, that would extend his sovereignty or advance his kingdom among men. One cannot imagine the Head of the church, which is his body, approving any segregation and discrimination within one of his churches.

Most churches welcome any who want to visit their worship services and their educational agencies and organizations. They welcome those of other faiths or of no faith, and in the vast majority of churches those of other cultural and racial groups are free to attend and at times are particularly honored. You know that what has been said is not true of one group in many churches. Many white churches would not welcome and some would not even admit a Negro as a visitor in a regular service. How can we justify the exclusion of the Negro from many and possibly most of our churches, which incidentally is true in the North as well as in the South? How can we explain this to ourselves? How can we explain it to fellow Negro Christians? What is more disturbing, how can we explain it to the Lord, who is the head of the church?

The church is or is supposed to be "the church of God" at Atlanta, Birmingham, or Houston. It would seem that God should say who comes into the fellowship of the church. The church is the body of Christ. As the head of the church it would seem that he and not a prejudiced minority or even a prejudiced majority should have the right to decide who comes in the door of the church and sits in the sanctuary that has been dedicated to him and to his worship. How terrible for any group that calls itself a church to tack a sign literally or figuratively across the front door to its building saying, "For white people only," or, "No Negroes admitted"! God does not have any such limiting signs for entrance into his family. God's church should not have any such signs, and it would seem that it cannot and will not have if it is really his church.

We might add, in a very specific way, that Christ, the head of his body, the church, is the only one who has the right to tell any church of his what to do about segregation and desegregation. This is not the right of the NAACP or of the White Citizens' Council. Neither is it the right of the pastor, the deacons, or in the deepest sense even of the congregation. It is the Lord's right alone. Our churches should honestly seek to know his will about this as about all other problems that they face.

How searching and disturbing is the statement by a great Negro Christian that most churches "are not churches of God but churches of men, of customs, and of tradition"![2]

A Fellowship

The idea of the church as a fellowship is rather prevalent in the New Testament. As an example, let us look again at Paul's introduction to his first letter to the Corinthians. There he reminds the Corinthians (1:9) that God is faithful, by whom they had been called into the "fellowship" or "partnership" "of," "with," or "belonging to" his Son. Whether the fellowship or partnership was and is "of," "with," or "belongs to" the Son, God is the one who has called them and calls us into that fellowship. All who share in that fellowship will dwell together in peace and harmony.

Paul, in marked contrast, turns from this fellowship, which belongs to Christ, to the dissensions at Corinth. His initial appeal to the Corinthians to heal or to eliminate their divisions was "by the name of our Lord Jesus Christ," or "by all that Christ means to you" (Phillips), or "for the sake of our Lord Jesus Christ" (Williams). Christ was the one with whom they had been brought into fellowship or partnership. If that fellowship was as vital as it should be there would not be, there could not be, dissensions and divisions among them. They would be united or "perfectly harmonious" (Williams) in their minds and judgments. Here is our hope for unity, for true fellowship. As we have fellowship with Christ, we shall have a sound and an abiding fellowship with all who belong to him.

Within this fellowship there is no place for any feeling of superiority or inferiority. The members of the group are to submit themselves to one another (Eph. 5:21). The strong are to serve the weak. They are to carry one another's burdens. Paul said to the Philippians, and would say to all who are in the Christian fellowship: "Stop act-

[2] Benjamin E. Mays in William S. Nelson (ed.), *The Christian Way in Race Relations* (New York, Harper, 1948), p. 222.

ing from motives of selfish strife or petty ambition but in humility practice treating one another as your superiors" (Phil. 2:3, Williams), or "Count others better than yourselves."

The fellowship within the churches of the New Testament was so meaningful that it led those who had possessions to share them with those who were in need. The idea of sharing is inherent in the word (*koinonia*) that is frequently translated "fellowship." The same word is variously translated "communication," "communion," "distribution," "partaker," and "sharing." Christian fellowship in the New Testament sense was no ephemeral something that had little if any relationship to the everyday realities of life. Membership in the fellowship carried "with it a responsibility for the welfare, physical as well as spiritual, of the other members of Christ's body."[3]

For New Testament Christians this spirit of shared responsibility carried far beyond the Jerusalem community. Paul as he visited the churches took an offering for the needy saints at Jerusalem (see Rom. 15:25–28; 1 Cor. 16:1–4). Thus, many Gentile Christians shared with Jewish Christians and possibly, to some degree, with those of other languages and nationalities.

Those who have been brought into the Christian fellowship through union with Christ are brethren. And brothers are brothers whether or not they like it. This is just as true in the spiritual as it is in the physical realm. Within the Christian family the common love of the children of God for their heavenly Father should cause them to love and live in peaceful fellowship with one another.

As a fellowship of or in the Spirit the church should demonstrate in its own fellowship the kind of world we would have if society itself were redeemed. The church is the germ or "the provisional showing-forth of God's ultimate intention for every segment of society." The world needs desperately a living demonstration of God's ideal or goal for human society. The church is the only institution that can give such a demonstration.

One element in that demonstration should be the fact that within the Christian fellowship there is no respect of persons. How could

[3] Tilson, *Segregation and the Bible*, p. 153.

there be when God is no respecter of persons, and the church is "the church of God"? Respect for persons, based on human external conditions, has no place in the fellowship of the Spirit.

James in his epistle applied the no-respecter-of-persons principle very specifically to the church. He related it in a definite way to only one area—to the church's treatment of the rich and the poor. However, both before and after his specific application of the principle to economic classes, James gave a general or an all-inclusive statement of the basic principle. His opening statement in the section is, "My brethren, hold not the faith of our Lord Jesus Christ, the Lord of glory, with respect of persons" (James 2:1 ASV). Mayor suggests the following meaning: "Do not you, who call yourselves believers in Christ, disgrace your faith by exhibitions of partiality."[4] Notice the plurals "persons" and "exhibitions." These plurals suggest that the principle of no partiality applies not only to the treatment of the wealthy and the poor but to any other man-established divisions of mankind.

Notice also the use of "my brethren" by James. There is something inconsistent about Christian brethren showing partiality. It violates the very foundations of brotherhood. The thing that made them brethren was their shared faith in the same Lord. As they hold fast their faith in Christ, they would not show any partiality. How could they when that faith was centered in the "Lord Jesus Christ"? Throughout his earthly journey Jesus had revealed repeatedly that he was no respecter of persons. How inconsistent with his spirit for a church of his to give preferential treatment to the rich simply because they are rich! It would be equally inconsistent for one of his churches to be partial to any other group—economic, social, cultural, national, or racial.

The One who was no respecter of persons while he walked among men is now "the Lord of glory." How incompatible for people to claim "to hold the faith of our Lord Jesus Christ, the Lord of glory" and at the same time to be partial in their treatment of his followers,

---

[4] Joseph B. Mayor, *The Epistle of St. James* (reprinted; Grand Rapids, Zondervan Publishing House, 1954), p. 79.

of those who hold the same faith! How incongruous for those who worship the Christ of glory to judge people on the basis of worldly carnal standards!

James, after his application of the principle to the treatment of the rich and poor in the meetings of the church, returns again to a statement of the general principle. Quite interestingly and significantly he relates it to love of neighbor, which he calls "the royal law."

Do we need to ask the question: Are our churches respecters of persons? Some may not be, but many and doubtlessly most of them are and hence they are under the condemnation of God, who is no respecter of persons. Many of those churches apply, at least in the fullest sense, the principle of respect for persons only to one group—the Negroes. Many of them, as suggested formerly, welcome to their worship services and into their membership those of all other cultural or racial groups.

A group of girls were going to a camp for a weekend outing. A Negro girl of about ten years of age asked the leader if she might go. The leader assured her that it would be all right with her and she was sure it would be with the other girls, but that she would need to check with the pastor and with the director of the camp. When she checked with them, they definitely and positively said, "No." Yet, in that group that weekend there were not only white girls, but also Oriental and Spanish-American girls. Why was the Negro girl denied the privilege? Why was she the only one to whom the camp was closed?

Many similar episodes could be given. There are some things that disturb a sensitive Christian when he hears of an incident like this. He wonders: How could that leader, how could the mother of that ten-year-old girl, how could her Sunday-school teacher, how could anyone explain to her what had happened? The question also inevitably arises: What effect will this experience have on her life and particularly upon her development as a child of God? Just as important: What will be its influence on the moral and spiritual lives of those other girls in that group? Do you ever wonder about these things?

Let us return again to the statement by James and let it search our hearts. Let us use Phillips' translation, which reads as follows: "Don't ever attempt, my brothers, to combine snobbery with faith in our Lord Jesus Christ!" (2:1). Again he says, "Once you allow any insidious distinctions to creep in, you are sinning, you have broken God's Law" (v. 9). Are we snobbish? Have we permitted any "insidious distinctions" to creep into our lives and into our churches?

The Churches: An Appraisal

In the main, the teachings and ideals we have sought to set out in this and preceding chapters are what the churches preach and teach. We will admit that some of the churches, at least some of their leaders and members, would not agree with the application that has been made of those teachings or principles to race relations. Also, we must frankly confess that most Christians and most churches have noticeably failed to practice what they have preached and professed to believe. Christians and churches should remember, however, and be grateful for the fact that the world judges them by their own standards, by the message they preach and teach. In other words, churches that preach an all-inclusive gospel, that have said that all men are created in the image of God, that Christ died for all, that all can come to Christ through faith, that God is no respecter of persons, and that all men are of equal worth and dignity in the sight of God and should be in the sight of men, the same churches will inevitably be judged by the world on the basis of what they preach.

Because of their basic message, the churches are increasingly embarrassed by segregation in general but particularly by the segregation pattern so persistently followed and at times defended within the Christian family. Segregation has been labeled "the great scandal in the church." There is a growing conviction, both outside and inside the churches, that there should be no Jim Crow churches. Possibly we should inject here the thought that although a church is all-white or all-Negro does not mean necessarily that it is a segregated church. Segregation, as defined previously, involves compulsion, either by law or by custom. There may be separated churches that are not segregated.

Segregation within the churches is a comparatively recent phenomenon. There is no indication of segregation, based on race or color, in the churches of the first centuries of the Christian era. The same was true in the Middle Ages. The basis for membership in a church was faith, not race; Christ, not color. The color bar in churches is a modern thing.

The separation of Negroes and whites in the churches of our country did not take place, on any large scale, until after the War between the States. Previously Negroes had been members with the white people. For example, one Baptist church in Charleston, South Carolina, had four hundred Negro members by 1804, while the First Baptist Church of Montgomery, Alabama, in 1865, had six hundred Negro members and only three hundred white members.[5] When the Southern Baptist Convention was organized in 1845, one report suggests that there were more Negro than white members of Baptist churches in proportion to the population.[6]

Let us come back to the contemporary picture. Although no reliable statistics seem to be available, it does seem that there are an increasing number of churches in Northern population centers that are interracial or biracial. There are also a number of predominantly white churches in Southern states, at least in states "with a Southern exposure," that have Negro members. Most of these are in educational centers. There are not many of these biracial churches, but they belong in the picture if that picture is to be complete.

Members of white churches should know that even if their churches opened their doors to Negroes, comparatively few would come to most of those churches. Like many other national, cultural, and racial groups, they seem, for various reasons, to prefer churches of their own. People generally tend to select a church that satisfies them socially, intellectually, emotionally, as well as spiritually.

[5] Walter L. Fleming, *Documentary History of Reconstruction* (reprinted; New York, Peter Smith, 1950), I, 244.
[6] Bertram Wilbur Doyle, *The Etiquette of Race Relations in the South* (Chicago, The University of Chicago Press, 1937), p. 37.

Some people, in appraising the situation regarding the churches and segregation, have unfortunately left the impression that the only churches that have done or that are willing to do anything about segregation are those that have become biracial in membership. Hundreds and even thousands of churches have never faced the situation in any tangible way. Many of those churches will not have to face the problem in a practical way in the foreseeable future. Some of them do not know what they would do if a spiritually qualified Negro sincerely presented himself for membership in the church. It is at least possible that some of those churches, if they had a chance or a challenge, would respond on the basis of the Christian ideal rather than on the basis of racial prejudice.

The more or less natural inclination of Negroes, as well as other groups, to be with their own people, along with the prevalence of residential separation or segregation in most communities, North and South, means that most white churches could formally or theoretically desegregate without experiencing any integration. In other words, for most white churches, even in the Deep South, the question of integration or an "inclusive membership" is, at least for the present, a purely hypothetical question. This does not mean, however, that such churches should not face up to the issue. A genuine willingness on the part of the members of a church to receive those of other races, including Negroes, into the fellowship of the church might do a great deal for the church, and would tremendously increase its influence for good in the world.

Segregation in the church violates something that is basic in the nature of the church. How can a church exclude from "the church of God" those who are children of God? How can it, as "the body of Christ," withhold the privilege of worship from those who have been brought into union with Christ? How can a group that claims to be a part of a fellowship of the Spirit refuse to share with any of the redeemed, or deny admission to its place of worship to those who seek that redemption? Unthinkable! Yes, unthinkable, and yet there are many groups that call themselves churches that are doing that very thing.

Let us repeat, however, that most Negroes evidently do not want to attend white churches; they do want the privilege to attend. The vast majority of them are not asking for membership in white churches; but they do not want that membership closed to them. They do not like, in the churches or anywhere else, signs reading, "No Trespassing," or, "No Negroes Allowed."

We must confess that there are churches, and they are not all in the South, that are thoroughly committed to the continuance of segregation in society and also within the church. Some of the leaders and members of these churches contend that segregation is in harmony with the ultimate or intentional will of God. We believe that such an attitude, which is the epitome of racial pride, cuts the very heart out of the Christian gospel and the Christian ethic. It imperils the soul of the church itself.

How tragic it would be if the churches became "the last bulwark of racial segregation"! What a paradox if secularism and secular institutions "outchristianize Christianity"! It has frequently been said that eleven o'clock on Sunday morning is the most segregated hour of the week. This is close enough to the truth to embarrass many of our churches and to give to many Christians an uneasy conscience.

Segregation itself will not be so bad as long as the "uneasy conscience" or "embarrassment" remains. As long as these continue there will be hope of improvement. It is a deep tragedy, however, when a segregated church is content with its segregation. How can such a church claim to be "the church of God"? How can it claim to speak for Christ?

The brighter side of the general church situation would be revealed by a reexamination of the pronouncements and statements by general church bodies, by the leaders of those bodies, and by ministerial groups. This was done, to some degree, in Chapter II. For a complete appraisal of the churches and segregation there would also need to be some consideration of the message the churches proclaim. This has likewise been done to some degree in former chapters. The preaching of the churches is admittedly much better than their practice. In spite of the failure of the churches, on such a large scale, to practice what they preach, the truth they preach performs a prophetic function in the society of men. There is certainly error mixed with the truth, but most churches proclaim enough of the truth of God to create a constructive tension not only between what they preach and what the world practices, but also between what they preach and what they themselves practice. It is this prophetic tension that is the main hope for progress toward God's purposes for his church and for the world. The work and ministry of the churches doubtlessly will be major factors in any progress of the future. One of the best assurances for progress within the Christian family itself is that the churches cannot escape their own message, with all of the implications of that message.

Possibly it should be stated that the Christian gospel has a message for an imperfect as well as a perfect situation. The churches should not only look for the kingdom to come but should work to extend the kingdom now. They have a message of alleviation and reconciliation as well as one of judgment and reconstruction. Even within a segregated society the churches have a mission to fulfill. They must seek to reach and to minister to people where they are. They must begin where the people are, if they are to lead them to where they ought to be. They cannot lead them where they ought to be, however, unless they maintain some tension in the direction they should go.

Parenthetically, it should be said that a complete and fair appraisal of the church and segregation would have to include a study of Negro churches. This is beyond the scope of this study which is written primarily for Christians of the white race. It is quite clear, however, that Negro churches and pastors are very active in the segregation-desegregation struggle. Negro ministers are providing much of the inspiration and leadership for their people. This fact may help to explain the moderation and self-restraint that has so far characterized most of the Negro's protests.

The Churches: Their Problems

Many people, some of them from within the Christian circle, have been and are very critical of the churches because of their failure to be a more positive factor in the segregation-desegregation controversy. They are particularly harsh in their criticism of the churches because of their failure to practice in their own fellowship what the gospel they preach so plainly teaches. We shall not seek to justify the failure of the churches, but we do believe that a clearer understanding of some of their problems would lead all of us to be more sympathetic with the churches and with their leaders.

Some people have pointedly contrasted the position and practice regarding segregation by the Roman Catholic Church and by Protestant groups, suggesting that the former has been much more Christian and consistent than the latter. While we do not want to deprecate what Roman Catholics have done, fairness demands that we examine the difference in the racial situation faced by Roman Catholicism and Protestantism in America.

Protestant churches have the problem of numbers, which is a major block to desegregation in school or church. For example, the Catholic Church claims in America approximately 31 million white adherents with less than 500,000 Negro members. In marked contrast, there are approximately 10 to 12 million Negro Protestants in the United States. The contrast is particularly sharp between the two largest white Protestant groups (Baptists and Methodists) in the United States and the Roman Church. More than 90 per cent of Negro Protestants belong to these two denominational families. There are in round numbers 7 million Negro Baptists and 10 million white Baptists. There are 2½ million Negro Methodists and about 8½ million white Methodists. There is a vast difference between the Catholic ratio of 62 to 1 and the Protestant ratio of 4 to 1, and still more difference between the Catholic ratio and the Baptist ratio, which is about 1½ to 1.

There is also a noticeable difference in the structure of the Roman Church and most Protestant groups. Rome speaks from the top down, although there have been a few places in the South, such as New Orleans, where the church officials have encountered considerable resistance from laymen to desegregation in the parochial schools and in the churches. The Catholic priest, however, gets his final authority from higher church officials and not from the people. His final appeal is to some papal encyclical. In contrast, the typical Protestant appeals to the Bible, but has no authoritative interpretation of the Bible. He is his own interpreter. It is true that the more one leans toward Rome, the more he tends to depend upon the church to decide for him what is right or wrong.

It is no mere accident that the local churches that are most completely controlled by the congregation, or are the most thoroughly democratic in their organization and government, are generally slower to change existing racial patterns. Such churches tend to be conservative along all lines. They move slowly. Even in Northern cities most churches that have desegregated and are following an inclusive membership program have done so without a vote by the congregation. Most of them have been churches whose polity did not require such a vote. Carrying the congregation along is one of the very real problems faced by many pastors of both the South and the North, who would like to do something about segregation within the churches.

It now seems that inclusive membership or desegregation within the churches will first come in churches in college and university towns and cities. This has already happened in a number of centers. It more than likely will come next in churches that minister largely to the middle and upper classes, to professional people, to the better educated. There may be noticeable exceptions to this pattern, but that seems to be the logical order or direction.

It has been implied that some of the problems the churches face in desegregating stem from their nature. A church is a divine-human institution. It is "the church of God," but it is "the church of God at Corinth" or at Charleston. As a human institution it suffers the inevitable limitations of its human nature. It is the institutional or organizational formulation of a great ideal, of a way of life. People should not be surprised that it falls short of that ideal. That is true of every effort to embody in a human institution or instrument any great concept or philosophy of life. For example, the so-called political democracies fall far short of the democratic dream. This failure, along with the church's failure to measure up to the demands of its divine nature, has created, in the main, the contemporary racial problem.

The divine-human nature of the church posits for it some of its most distressing problems but also some of its most glorious opportunities. Its commission and its message come from the Lord, but it is commissioned to "go into all the world" and the message is to be delivered for God to the people of the world. Those people have all the temptations and limitations of the fleshly nature. Furthermore, the church ministers to those individuals in a particular environment, which inevitably will affect their lives and attitude, and hence will affect the life of the church itself. No church can escape its environment or keep from being influenced, to some degree, by that environment. This was true of the church at Corinth and the other churches to which Paul wrote. It will be true of churches in Chattanooga and in Chicago, in Dallas and in Detroit, in Louisville and in Los Angeles, in New Orleans and in New York. However, no church should be a slave to its environment. It should lift its constituency toward God. It cannot do that if it completely makes its peace with the world, getting its standards from the world rather than from the living God.

As a human institution, the church is frequently under pressure from its members, and from people outside the church, to conform to community patterns and practices. One function the church is supposed to perform for its members and for the community is to maintain a constant tension toward the Christian ideal for the individual and for the world. It is true that if the tension becomes too great between what the church preaches and what the community practices, the church may lose its opportunity to minister to the community and to the people of the community.

The preceding warning is not needed by many churches. It may be needed by some pastors and church leaders. Just how far and fast they can go in applying the perfect Christian ideal to an imperfect world is one of their most perplexing and sometimes frustrating problems. The problem is particularly acute just now in the area of race. How can they serve the cause of Christ best: by going full length right now or by keeping the pressure gently but firmly in the right direction? No one who does not live with the problem from day to day can fully understand or appreciate the seriousness of this problem for many sensitive Christian souls.

Some of the problems the churches are having in the area of race stem from their own failures and mistakes. Space will permit a consideration of only one or two of these failures. The present racial crisis has made it crystal clear that many churches have been more interested in quantity of members than in quality of membership. They have made it too easy for people to become and to remain church members. Not enough has been expected of the members. Civic clubs and fraternal orders have frequently been more demanding of their members than the churches. This should not be true.

There also has been a tendency to separate evangelism from ethics and church membership from daily Christian living. Many people tend to measure the religion of church members too exclusively in formalistic terms. They believe that the good Christian is one who attends the services of his church regularly and gives liberally to the support of its program. A good Christian should and will do these things, but one may be meticulously faithful to the forms of religion and yet fail to be a good Christian. Really, faithfulness to formalities may be used as a substitute for vital Christian living.

Whatever may be the reason, many churches, in the contemporary crisis, are paying dearly for their failure to maintain quality of membership and to lead their members to understand what it means to live the Christian life. They are discovering that many of their members, who are mature in years and who have been members of the church for many years, are still babes in Christ. Their immaturity has been revealed to a marked degree in their attitudes during the present racial crisis. Many of them have revealed that they are more Southerners than Christians. They refuse to see the relevance of the great truths of the Christian faith to the racial situation, or, seeing their relevance, they have refused to conform to them. Far too many of them evidently have not progressed in their commitment to Christ as Lord of their lives.

Let us say again, however, that the main hope for the churches and for the world is in the message of the churches. It challenges the churches and their members as it also challenges the world and the people of the world. Ultimately the churches, as well as the world, must come to terms with that message. There are signs that there is a stirring within the churches. Churches and church leaders are being plagued with an uneasy conscience. One way to ease such a conscience is to practice what is preached or to bring conduct into line with that which disturbs the conscience. The disturber, in this case, is the central core of the gospel message.

CHAPTER EIGHT

Segregation and World Missions

The first impulse when a man comes into the family of God through union with Christ is to invite others to share that experience with him. Likewise, it is natural for a church, composed of those who have been brought into union with Christ, to want to share with other peoples the blessings its members have found in him. This is one motivation, though not the only one, for the Christian missionary movement.

The missionary passion which was so vibrant in the New Testament churches and in the Christian movement in the early centuries was lost, to a large degree, for many centuries. The church, at least as represented by the main stream of the Christian movement, seemed to become more interested in her worldly power than in her spiritual witness to the world. She was more concerned with her own welfare than promoting the kingdom of God among men. Even the Reformation, with all the inner renewal that it brought, did not recapture, except in a very limited way, the missionary passion of the early church.

The modern missionary movement dates from William Carey, who went to India in 1793. It is no accident that the modern missionary advance was so closely related to the expansion of world trade. This world trade, which stemmed from the development of commercial and industrial capitalism and which has noticeably influenced at least indirectly the missionary movement, centered primarily in Europe and later in the United States. It has been from these two, particularly from the latter in more recent years, that the representatives of the Christian movement have gone around the world. This means that most of those representatives have been and are white people, and that a majority of them have gone to the colored peoples of the world. These companion facts have tremendous significance for any study, from the Christian viewpoint, of segregation and desegregation.

The Commission of the Churches

One impelling motive that has led the churches to give of their monies and of their sons and daughters to carry the message of Christ around the world has been the conviction that the parting words of Christ, "Go, therefore . . ." were not only for the group of disciples to whom he spoke, but for all who have succeeded them as his disciples. That commission has never been repealed. Christians and churches may forget, or fail to heed, but the resurrected Christ continues to speak.

The continuing message of Christ is "Go . . . make disciples of *all nations.*" We may fail to have inclusive churches in the homeland, but the commission is inclusive. The book of Acts spells out the commission rather specifically: "You shall be my witnesses ["witnesses for me," Williams] in Jerusalem and in all Judea and Samaria and to the end of the earth" (Acts 1:8). They were to be his witnesses or witnesses for him. They were to tell others what they knew by actual experience with him. They were to be his witnesses in Jerusalem and in Judea, but notice that despised "Samaria" was also included. In harmony with the commission in Matthew, the record in Acts emphasizes the very end of the earth. No corner of the world and no group in that world were to be neglected.

The disciples who heard the risen Christ give his commission understood, although rather imperfectly, "that their sphere of labor was to be coextensive with the world." In response to his command they went everywhere turning the world upside down. One reason for the marvelous missionary effectiveness of these early Christians was the deep sense of mission and purpose which gripped not only a small minority but a big majority of them. They had not developed the rather sharp division and the marked contrast between the clergy and the laity which soon crept into the Christian movement and which has continued to plague and to limit it. This unscriptural distinction is one of the reasons for the contemporary cleavage between many ministers and their laymen regarding the race issue.

Not only did most of the disciples in the early church have a deep sense of personal mission, but increasingly they saw more clearly the inclusiveness of the commission of Christ. It required a vision on a housetop to lead Peter to open the door of the gospel to Cornelius, a Gentile. It required a vision on the Damascus Road to prepare God's Apostle to the Gentiles. God, however, was equal to the occasion, and his chosen vessels were responsive to his call.

Let us return for a moment to Acts 1:8. Notice that before the disciples were to be Christ's witnesses, they were to receive power. That power would come when the Holy Spirit ("the promise of my Father," Luke 24:49) came upon them. When the Spirit came on the day of Pentecost, the disciples immediately began to fulfill the command or commission of Christ to be his witnesses.

There are two or three lessons or implications for contemporary Christians and churches in this experience. We are to tarry until the power comes upon us, but once the power comes, once we feel the touch of the divine Spirit on our spirits, we are to go in the strength of that power to witness for Christ. Also, if the Spirit really possesses us and lives in us, we shall be willing to go to the ends of the earth, which will mean to any man or woman in need of our witnessing in Jerusalem, in Judea, and even in our Samaria. If we are led and empowered by the Spirit of God, we will not set limits for our witnessing. Just as it is true that the Christian movement "must be active at the extremities, or it becomes chilled at the heart," so a local church or an individual Christian must be active at the extremities or the very heart of the Christian faith will be chilled. This is a fundamental spiritual law. And those extremities may be social and cultural as well as geographic.

The disciples were not only commanded or commissioned to go

unto all nations or to the end of the earth, they were also commanded to teach those who were enlisted as disciples, or learners, all that Christ had commanded them. They were not only to teach them to know what he had taught, but to be obedient to or "to practice" what he had commanded. The latter is infinitely more difficult than the former, although one never knows anything in the truest sense until he has honestly sought to practice it.

The Christian missionaries who have gone around the world have followed, in the main, this twofold injunction. They have sought to make disciples, and then to instruct those disciples in the way of the Lord. They have done the latter because they have recognized that when one becomes a follower of Christ he is a babe in Christ. He must be nurtured. An important element in that nurturing process is consistent, persistent instruction in the things Christ taught.

It is possible that the things Christ had commanded his disciples included some things that are not recorded in the gospels. There is enough recorded, however, to challenge us and our churches to the end of life's journey. This will certainly be true if we seek honestly to follow the leadership of the Spirit of God in our lives. He will constantly reveal to us deepening insights into the truth taught by Jesus and revealed in his life.

The Peoples of the World

According to the statistical office of the United Nations, the population of the world was distributed as follows by midyear, 1956:

Africa	220,000,000
America (North)	245,000,000
America (South)	129,000,000
Asia (excluding the U.S.S.R.)	1,512,000,000
Europe (excluding the U.S.S.R.)	412,000,000
Oceania	15,000,000
U.S.S.R.	200,000,000
Grand Total	2,733,000,000

Notice that considerably over half of the peoples of the world live in Asia, with an additional 220 million in Africa. Practically all of these peoples are colored; at least they are nonwhite. There are other large segments of colored peoples in other sections of the world. Possibly not more than 25 to 30 per cent of the people of the world could be classified as white or Caucasian.

It has been estimated that the human race is increasing by 88,000 each day, which would mean an annual increase of approximately 32 million. The world population doubled in the two centuries from 1650 to 1850 and again in one century from 1850 to 1950. If the present rate of increase continues, which is doubtful, the world population will double again within the next fifty years. Of the present annual increase of approximately 32 million, 20.5 millions of that increase are in Asia and Africa, where the great mass of the colored peoples of the world lives.

The geographic distribution, which is also largely racial, of the population of the world has major significance for the West, for the United States, and for the Christian movement with its world perspective. The white man of the West should remember that he is in the minority in the world. He may control the power now, but there is no assurance he will in the future. He should know and the governments that he controls should know that the great underprivileged masses, most of whom are the colored peoples of the world, are restless. They are on the march in Asia, Africa, and around the world. This march seems to be one of those inevitably revolutionary movements that will sweep before it anything and everything that seeks to stop it. It can be guided and possibly delayed, but the march irresistibly proceeds.

One cannot understand the contemporary racial situation in the United States apart from this restless movement among the masses. The Negroes in America, and to a lesser degree other minority groups, are increasingly catching step with the moving masses in Africa, Asia, and elsewhere.

It is the movement of the masses that is rapidly bringing an end to colonialism around the world. Old colonial empires have tottered and fallen. We have seen this happen in recent years. We are seeing it happen today in Asia and in Africa. Bishop Rajah B. Manikam, of the

Tamil Evangelical Lutheran Church of South India, in a recent address at the Divinity School of Yale University, said that the French and Russian revolutions are dwarfed in comparison with the changes taking place in Asia and Africa today. He further said: "Never before have so many millions of people taken part in such a rapid and radical social upheaval. In the last ten years, nearly 700 millions have gained their independence." There has been an awakening of pride in race and class. This helps to explain the rise of Arab "nationalism" in the Middle East and the growing sense of independence among the peoples of the Orient and the Dark Continent.

This growing restlessness among the masses should not surprise the peoples of the West. For many years the Western industrial countries have been exploiting the natural resources of Asia, the Middle East, and Africa. They have also been exporting to those areas their manufactured products. A nation or a region cannot export its manufactured products, it cannot have commerce with another area of the world without some exchange of ideas. Some of the basic concepts that have provided the foundation for Western civilization were inevitably exported to other countries and their peoples.

There are several of those basic concepts, but no one is more central in the Western way of life than respect for the human person. The individual, at least from the theoretical viewpoint, has been considered the supreme value. Political systems and economic orders are supposed to serve him. He is the point of reference in every aspect of Western life.

It seems that in recent years the peoples of the Orient and Africa have begun to take seriously this basic concept, along with the freedoms that it implies. They have desired to move up the human ladder and share more equitably in the good things of life. They are seeking for themselves more of a share in the food and freedom of the world. They are demanding that they be respected and treated as fellow human beings. They are not only unwilling to be ruled over by the white man, they are also rejecting any paternalistic approach to their problems.

There are plenty of evidences that these restless masses are helping to shape the present and may shape the future even more. The leaders of the world, for good or bad, in recent years have been those who have sensed the stirring among the masses, white as well as colored, and have sought to capture or to cooperate with the marching masses. This helps to explain the rise and in some cases the decline of such divergent personalities as Hitler, Mussolini, Stalin, Roosevelt, Khrushchev, Mao Tse-tung, Gandhi, Nehru, and Nasser. The movement among the underprivileged masses, most of whom are colored, also helps to explain the influence of the Asian-African bloc of nations in general and in the United Nations in particular. On some issues this bloc has provided a balance between the East and the West.

The Christian missionary movement must share the responsibility for the restless movement of the masses, particularly in Asia and Africa. It has been a disturber of the accustomed ways from William Carey's day until today. It has challenged the old ways not only in the life of the individual but also in his society. The missionary realizes, possibly more fully than other Christians, that the gospel is the power or the dynamite of God. It is a tremendously revolutionary force. It is new wine and it cannot be contained in old wine skins. It may be that the failure of many Christian missionary leaders to recognize this last fact has helped to pave the way for the rise and spread of communism in the Orient, particularly in China. With few exceptions, the missionaries seemingly failed to understand that the basic concepts of the Christian faith demanded a new social structure. Communism has taken advantage of this failure and in China, as elsewhere, it has built on a foundation that had been prepared or laid by the Christian movement.

One concept which was a part of that foundation and an important factor in the stirring among the masses was and is the idea of the dignity and worth of the human person. This concept, which, as stated earlier, is so central in the Western way of life, is very explicitly taught by the missionaries. The gospel they preach and teach says that all men are created in the image of God, that Christ died for all, that the way to salvation is open to all, that God is no respecter of persons, that all who come into the family of God through faith are brothers in Christ.

These teachings of the Christian missionaries have been far more influential among many of the peoples of Asia and Africa than the number of converts would suggest. In some countries, such as China, a considerable number of the top-level leaders were either Christians or had been trained in church-related schools and hence had been exposed to basic Christian teachings.

The contribution of the missionaries to the march of the masses was a by-product of their work. The main interest of most of them was to bring men and women into right relation with God through faith in Christ. In other words, their primary approach to their work was evangelistic.

However, when one is brought into a vital union with the living Christ his life's perspective is changed. This is true whether he lives in Africa or Atlanta, in China or Chicago, in Japan or Jacksonville, in India or Indianapolis, in Latin America or Louisville. One who has been made a new creation in Christ Jesus changes his attitude toward himself and toward others as well as toward God. He is no longer satisfied just to exist. His relation to God gives to him purpose and drive in his life. His new relationship creates within him not only a deeper sense of his own dignity and worth, but it also helps him to see more clearly and to appreciate more fully the worth and dignity of all other men. All of this is a major contribution to the movement among the masses of the world. This is just as true of the masses in America as it is in Asia and Africa. We had better understand that the march of the masses in every part of the world is closely related. Those masses are feeling for and with one another. Mistreatment anywhere creates resentment among them everywhere.

The Challenge of Communism

The Christian movement in its world missionary program still faces the challenge of the indigenous religions of the various sections of the world. There has been a revival of interest in some of them, such as Hinduism and Buddhism, in some areas. The most marked renewal, however, has been in Mohammedanism or Islam. Christian missionaries have not only found it difficult to make progress among Moslems, they also are being actively challenged by them in some areas, particularly in sections of Africa. There are approximately half as many Moslems (416 million) in the world as professed followers of Christ of all major faiths (820 million), with many more Moslems than Protestants (250 million).

There has arisen in the contemporary period, however, a movement which is possibly the most formidable foe the Christian movement has ever faced. This foe, communism, challenges Christianity at home, but particularly on foreign mission fields. Its program is to win the world, and to win the world it believes that it must win the marching masses, who may hold the secret to the future destiny of the world. Thus, around the world the battle is on—not only between the representatives of the West and communism but also between Christ's representatives and those of communism. And Christ's representatives should never be identified with those of the West. We may be strong believers in democracy and even in the so-called free-enterprise economic system, but let us beware of ever identifying Christianity with any political system or economic order. Such identification will be, as it has been, a serious handicap to the missionary movement in its struggle with communism for the minds and souls of the peoples of the world.

The leaders of communism have evidently sensed the direction in which the masses are moving and are seeking to capitalize on that movement. Those masses are wanting food, freedom, and respect, along with a sense of purpose. Communism promises to give to them all of these things. What it does not tell the peoples of the world is that it cannot satisfy the deeper hungers of the human spirit. Neither does it tell them that what it promises to do for them it will not and possibly cannot do. It promises to them freedom but ultimately it will enslave them. It promises to them respect and a sense of worth and dignity. It does not say that in communism the individual exists only as an instrument. He does not possess independent worth. It is the mass man that is exalted. And that mass man can be equated with the Party and its program. The individual is of value only as he serves the purposes of the mass man, as he promotes the program of the Party.

Communism is a creation of the contemporary world crisis as much as it is a creator of it. Conditions in Asia and Africa, but particularly in the former, have been made to order for communism. Whatever may be the reason for the rise and rapid spread of communism, the opening words of the Communist Manifesto, written by Marx and Engels in 1848, that "a spectre is haunting Europe—the spectre of Communism," could be expanded to read, "A spectre is haunting the world—the spectre of Communism."

That specter that haunts the West and the world has been labeled by Arnold Toynbee as a heresy of the West. It was born in the West, was adopted by the Russians, and has become an international movement that has come back to plague the West. It has been particularly adept at pointing out the evident weaknesses of the West, weaknesses which stem, in the main, from its failure to live up to its basic principles or concepts. Nowhere is this weakness more evident than in the failure of the democracies to apply consistently their democratic principles to the minorities in their midst. This failure has been most evident, at least in recent years, regarding the Negro, the largest minority group in the United States. This failure has become, from the viewpoint of the colored peoples of the world, our Achilles' heel. No one is more conscious of this fact than the Christian missionaries, most of whom work among the colored peoples of the world.

What communism has done for democracy it has also done, to a considerable degree, for Christianity. It has consistently pointed up the failure of the contemporary organized forms of Christianity to practice what they preach. It has done this in an effective way in the backward areas of the world, in the sections where most Christian missionaries work. Rightly or wrongly, the communists suggest that Christianity is a movement for the privileged, and not for the under-privileged. They declare that it is used as an instrument by the ruling or controlling classes in the Western nations to keep the underprivileged down and themselves in power. They charge that "religion is the opium of the people," an expression which was coined by Marx.

There is no one area where the communists are pointing out more persistingly the failure of the churches than in the field of race relations. They are saying, particularly to the colored masses of the world, that the Christian missionaries preach brotherhood and the equality of all men in the sight of God, but that the country and the churches that send them out are failing to practice, in relation to the Negro, what they preach. If the churches of America were taking a positive stand against segregation within the Christian family and in society in general, then the missionaries would have an answer for the communist. But what can they say when many of the very churches that send them out and support them are slaves to the racial pattern of the environment in which they find themselves rather than challengers of that pattern?

In spite of all of this, there are many people, including some church members, who are charging that the movement to desegregate the schools and the churches is a communistic plot. They loosely label anyone who supports desegregation as a communist. Such labeling is a common technique, used largely by little minds and little people when they cannot answer a question or cannot oppose on an intelligent basis any program or movement.

We should see that the continuance and particularly the defense of segregation plays right into the hands of the communists. They are out to capture the marching masses everywhere in the world, evidently believing that those masses represent "the wave of the future." Segregation of peoples on the basis of class or color provides a major plank in the strategy of the communists to win the masses. It is to their advantage for the pattern of prejudice and discrimination to continue so that they will have a continuing occasion to denounce both the West and the Christian movement for their hypocrisy.

One reason for the strength of the challenge of communism to the Christian missionary movement is the fact that it is not only a Western heresy but also a Christian heresy. At least it includes "a deposit of

Christian influence of great importance."[1] Toynbee speaks of communism as "a latter-day religion," as "a leaf taken from the book of Christianity—a leaf torn out and misread,"[2] while it was Oswald Spengler who said that Christianity was the grandmother of Bolshevism. Harold Laski, the former intellectual leader of the British Labor Party, once said that the "profoundly religious character" of communism was the secret to its tremendous dynamic.[3]

The Burden of the Missionaries

The representatives of world missions bear many burdens. Here our concern will be restricted to the burden of segregation at home. We cannot fully understand the weight of that burden unless we understand that the vast majority of missionaries, who go from the United States to the other peoples of the world, work among the nonwhite or colored peoples. For example, of the missionaries who serve under the Division of World Missions of the Methodist Church, 29 per cent work with Negro people and 58 per cent with other colored peoples. The remaining work in countries, particularly in Latin America, "where a certain segment of the population is classified as 'white' to differentiate it from Negro, Indian, and other colored elements."[4]

What is true of the Methodist Church is true of most other Protestant groups. The American Board of Commissioners for Foreign Missions reports 25 per cent of its missionaries in Africa, with 12 per cent in Japan, 16 per cent in India and Ceylon, and an additional 10 per cent in the Philippines and Micronesia. The others (37 per cent) work in Europe and the Near East. The United Christian Missionary Society of the Disciples of Christ reports that 16 per cent of its missionaries work with Negro people in the Belgian Congo, Jamaica, and South Africa, with most of the others working with other colored

[1] John C. Bennett, *Christianity and Communism* (New York, Association Press, 1948), p. 46.
[2] *Civilization on Trial* (New York, Oxford University Press, 1948), p. 236.
[3] *The Dilemma of Our Times* (London, George Allen and Unwin, 1952), p. 205.
[4] Letter from Theodore Runyan, July 22, 1958.

peoples. The United Church of Christ, formerly the Evangelical and Reformed Church, has 26 per cent of its missionaries serving colored people in Africa, with the vast majority of the others serving in the Orient. Rather interestingly, one Negro was serving in Japan as a missionary under appointment of the Church's Board of International Missions. The Protestant Episcopal Church reports that 11 of its 230 missionaries on the field are Negroes. "These are in good and full standing as missionaries of our Board."[5]

The Foreign Mission Board of the Southern Baptist Convention had a total of 1,186 missionaries under appointment in 1958. Of this number 264, or 22.3 per cent, were serving in Africa and 367, or 30.9 per cent, in the Orient. This would mean that 631 missionaries were serving in Asia and Africa, or 53.2 per cent of the total number under appointment. There were 38 additional missionaries serving in Hawaii, most of whose peoples are Orientals. There were 4 in the Bahamas and 2 in Jamaica. With the exception of 49 missionaries in the Middle East and 29 in Europe, the remainder were in Central and South America. Many of those countries have a considerable Indian and Negro population.

When we realize that such a large percentage of missionaries work among the colored peoples of the world, we can understand their deep concern about our treatment of the Negroes in the States. As suggested earlier, the masses with whom the missionaries work are on the move. They are restless. They are also tending to identify the struggles of colored peoples elsewhere with their own struggle for more of a place in the life and work of the world. There is definitely a tendency for all of the colored peoples of the world to join ranks in a common cause. This means that the people of Asia, Africa, and elsewhere are very sensitive to the treatment of the Negro in the United States.

Most of the missionaries who do not work exclusively with colored people work where there is some mixture of population. In these areas the churches are not segregated. In Latin America, for example, where there are many Indians and in some countries a large number

[5] Letter from the Rev. Claude L. Pickens, Jr., July 25, 1958.

of Negroes, the churches are not segregated. In other words, the denominations, even those most definitely and exclusively Southern, do not practice segregation where they do mission work. It is hard for the peoples of those countries to understand why we would practice one thing on the mission field and something drastically different at home.

The modern methods of communication, which have made the world into one neighborhood, or "one great whispering gallery," have tremendously increased the missionaries' problems. Now the peoples of the world know tomorrow what happens anywhere in the world today. A missionary on furlough from East Africa expressed it as follows: "What happens in Little Rock today is in tomorrow's papers in East Africa. And tomorrow comes seven hours earlier there than here." A picture of a white man kicking a Negro during a disturbance over school desegregation that appeared in the afternoon papers in the States was published the next morning on the front page of a leading paper in São Paulo, Brazil. Mob action to prevent Negro young people from attending the high school in Mansfield, Texas, a small community close to Fort Worth, made the headlines in a daily paper of Cali, Colombia. When a prominent Southern minister spoke out in defense of segregation, a missionary from Nigeria, in West Africa, said that a report of his speech would be on the front page of every paper in Nigeria the next day. The people to whom the missionaries go with the gospel formerly considered only the validity of the gospel itself. Now they demand that the gospel be validated by the lives of the folks who send it to them. The missionary's task is doubly hard in these days of racial tension.

The racial situation at home creates problems for the representative of world missions even as he goes for the first time to his field of service. Most of those missionaries have grown up in a segregated society. They have been taught many of the prejudices that are a part of their social heritage. Most of them have attended and have been trained in churches that maintain and at least tacitly defend the segregation pattern. Yet the majority of these Christian young people go to work with colored peoples. Many of them testify that they have had to make major adjustments in their thinking concerning and their attitude toward the peoples of other races before they could become effective missionaries. Those who do not make the adjustments either come home after a while, or seek to live a somewhat isolated life and render a sort of paternalistic type of service. This latter group provides an unduly large proportion of the missionaries who break in health, or for other reasons ultimately have to come home. Some of them are practically forced from the field because of the failure of the people to accept them. In contrast, those who are free from prejudice, or get rid of it, love the people and in turn are loved by them. The people of the Congo said of one missionary, "His skin is white but his heart is black." That was their way of saying that he was one of them.

Regardless of how successful the missionary's personal adjustment may have been, he still faces the pressures that the racial situation at home creates for him. In most sections of the world his "white" skin is no longer an asset but a liability to him as Christ's ambassador. That white skin is identified with the exploiter, with the oppressor. His color is frequently a psychological block or barrier that he must overcome.

The remainder of this chapter, in the main, will be direct or indirect quotations from the representatives of world missions. Most of these will be men and women who are at work among the colored peoples of Asia and Africa. A few statements of missionary executives or regional directors of missionary service will be included. Some will be identified by name, others, for various reasons, will remain anonymous.

Ross Coggins, a young missionary on his first tour of duty in Indonesia, is the author of the following poem, which is directly related to some things we have been saying:

> Would God that friends of segregation
>   For awhile could leave our nation,
> Come with me across the seas,
>   Work by my side with Javanese;

Or, if not here, some other clime
Where Christ is preached—Oh, just one time!

But, lacking means of transmigration
And knowing well the limitation
Of mere words upon a page,
These lines are framed: the world will gauge
The light we lift by darkness driven
From countries whence this faith is given.

In times of swift communication,
Nation cannot hide from nation
What it does. Within brief hours
Headlines shout how hatred's powers
Close love's doors with jarring thud
Because of race, because of blood.

A helpless, dark-skinned boy is slain,
His slayers freed to slay again;
No mark of Cain upon their brow,
They strut in triumph and avow,
"If a nigger is my brother,
Let his keeper be another."

Is there no love that will transcend
Man's petty strife and condescend
To men of other creed and hue?
Forgive! They know not what they do!
Is it too much, we humbly ask—
Unchain our hands to do our task.

The last line sums up the plea of Christ's missionaries around the world. For them, racial segregation and discrimination are chains that handcuff; they are extra burdens on their backs.

The same young missionary recently said: "The most dangerous area of our vulnerability is that of race relations. It is this problem which is the delight of our enemies and the dismay of the missionary." E. Luther Copeland, a professor of missions in a theological seminary who himself served as a missionary in the Orient, similarly has said: "The missionary movement carries about its neck the mighty millstone of our inconsistency as it operates in the colored world, and it staggers more and more beneath this weight."

The converts of world missions cannot understand our inconsistency. They are perplexed. How can Christian people in the States send to them a gospel of love and redemption, and yet refuse to accept into their fellowship at home those who have been saved through that gospel? Sometimes those of us who live in the States are also perplexed. How can men give willingly and possibly occasionally sacrificially to missions, and then "defend a social system which invalidates the missionary message"? John E. Mills of Nigeria wrote back to the States saying that we "must quickly come to the place where we treat all men on the basis of their individual worth, or else we must pull down our missionary banners and leave the carrying out of the gospel to others who will do so." Another, writing from the Orient, said: "You would just have to be here to know how tragic is the effect of racial bigotry at home on the work of the missionary." Bud Dozier, a young missionary doctor, summed up the matter by saying that on the mission field there is absolute intolerance of segregation. He also said that the greatest criticism the missionaries have to face stems from segregation at home, in the institutions and in the churches from which they come.

The missionaries are constantly prodded by questions from Christians as well as from non-Christians. How would you have answered an Indonesian university student who asked the following questions in a discussion period during a church youth week: "Everyone wants freedom in life. But why does discrimination still exist in a religious country like America on the Negro race? On what points do Christians agree and disagree with it?" A mature missionary in Indonesia, Buford L. Nichols, who served a number of years in China before he and his family were forced to leave during World War II, recently said: "These islands besiege me almost daily with questions about this issue." The "issue" he spoke of was segregation in America. He said that whether or not America will "maintain the friendship and respect of the nations of the world depends largely on the outcome of this issue."

This same missionary, in another communication—a letter that protested a rather weak answer, in a church publication, to a question concerning segregation, said:

We must view this matter of segregation from a broad angle. We must take an all-American view, a world view, a Christian view. Sectionalism must not cramp our Christian convictions nor dim our better vision.

. . . .

I tell the people here that segregation is not Christian. I believe it with all my soul.

Nichols was born in the South and received his education in Southern institutions.

M. T. Rankin, a real missionary statesman, who was imprisoned for some years by the Japanese during World War II, sometime before his death summed up the whole matter as follows:

More and more the sincerity of our missionary interest in the colored peoples in their native lands will be judged by our attitudes and actions toward the people of those lands who live among us.

One of the most delicate and difficult tasks of the missionary is to try to prepare the colored convert who is going to the States. It is particularly embarrassing when he has to explain to him that he will not be welcomed into many of the churches that sent the missionary to his people. A young reporter on a West Indian newspaper told Robert G. Nelson, the Executive Secretary of the Department of Africa of the United Christian Missionary Society, how much he and his people had appreciated having the missionaries live with them. He then asked the disturbing question, "What would happen if I were to visit your churches in the United States?"

The President of the Nigerian Baptist Convention, S. A. Lawoyin, could give an answer to the question. While in the United States, he was invited to speak in a white church in the South. He arrived early and was ushered around to the back door "and into a cubby hole until time to mount the pulpit to tell of God's love and the love of those who had come to tell him the story."

Similar incidents could be multiplied. We shall give just one other. A native of Nigeria was enrolled as a student in a Southern theological seminary, from which he later received its highest degree —a doctorate in theology. His wife had to have surgery during the time. She was refused admission, because she was a Negro, to a hospital owned by the denomination to which she and her husband belonged. She had to go to a Catholic hospital. They both suffered many other indignities while they were in the States, yet this talented couple went back to Nigeria with no evidence of bitterness or malice and spoke appreciatively of the many courtesies that were extended to them while in the States.

One of the clearest statements on the whole race issue and its effects on world missions is one that was adopted unanimously by the Nigerian Mission of Southern Baptists. This statement was sent to the Foreign Mission Board of the Southern Baptist Convention with a request that it be made available to the people. It reads as follows:

Nigerians are acutely conscious of the problems of race relations in America, they identify themselves with the American Negro, and they consider racism in any form unjust.

We believe that racism is inconsistent with, and a hindrance to, the world mission task to which Southern Baptists have committed themselves.

We sincerely commend Southern Baptist individuals and institutions for the rapid progress made in recent years toward elimination of racism, and for the service they have rendered in meeting the spiritual, educational, and social needs of all men.

We urge all Southern Baptists to work toward the solution of racial problems, realizing that only as these problems are solved can the Great Commission be carried out fully. A major obstacle is the fact that some Southern Baptist institutions do not accept Negroes (which includes Nigerians), and we urge the authorities of these institutions to give special attention to this problem in the light that we, your representatives to Africa, have been commissioned to share with Africans, the gospel of Jesus Christ.

Miss Antonia Canzoneri, missionary nurse of Nigeria, is the source for the following poem. The author is unknown.

AFRICA

I slept, I dreamed, I seemed to climb a hard, ascending track
And just behind me labored one whose face was black.
I pitied him, but hour by hour he gained upon my path.

He stood beside me, stood upright, and then I turned in wrath,
"Go back," I cried, "What right have you to stand beside me here?"
I paused, struck dumb with fear, for lo! the black man was not there—
But Christ stood in his place!
And oh! the pain, the pain, the pain that looked from that dear face.

It is Cornell Goerner, a former missions professor and now regional secretary for Europe, the Middle East and Africa, who has said that there is "no way to avoid the race factor in world missions, except by rising above it in Christian love." Are we rising above it in Christian love in our own lives? Are we helping our churches to rise above it? Are we part of the problem or are we part of the solution for the problem? Are we adding burdens to the backs of our missionaries, or are we seeking to lighten those burdens?

CHAPTER NINE

Conclusion:
A Statement of Convictions

In the preceding chapters we have sought progressively to present the Christian ideal concerning segregation and desegregation. The first chapters were somewhat factual. The last chapters have been more pointedly Christian in their emphasis. In this concluding chapter we want to present or restate as concisely and clearly as possible some personal convictions.

The Christian ideal would demand the elimination of all segregation, by law or custom, based on class or color. This is true because segregation, which inevitably means discrimination, is contrary to the spirit and teachings of Jesus. It violates the very heart of the message proclaimed by the churches. That message says that God is the creator of all, that Christ died for all, that God is no respecter of persons, and that man as man is of infinite value. This value is derived from man's relation, real or potential, to God, and is not dependent on outer circumstances such as economic condition, cultural level, or color of skin.

Segregation in society is bad enough; it is worse when practiced within the church which is supposed to be the church of God, the body of Christ, the family of the redeemed. Whenever it is practiced within the Christian body, the divine nature of the church with its divine mission and message has been overshadowed by its human

163

nature. Segregation within the church violates something basic in its life. The contemporary church cannot witness effectively to a world in sin, unless it rids itself of the sin of segregation within its own fellowship.

The preceding means that our churches should reexamine their own practices in the whole area of human relations and in the area of racial segregation in particular. They should open their hearts and ears to the Word of the Lord. They should seek the leadership of the Spirit of God as they attempt to find the will of God regarding this perplexing problem. They should recognize that the churches have a prophetic ministry to perform, that they are to speak the Word of the Lord to the peoples of the world. They should also know that what they practice within their own fellowship will speak much more clearly and forcibly than what they say. This means that our churches as rapidly as possible should rid themselves of all segregation within their ranks. They should do this because of the effects it will have upon them and their witness at home and abroad, but they should do it primarily because they are persuaded that segregation is wrong, that it is contrary to the purpose of God.

Even though all segregation might be eliminated, there could still be separated churches or distinctively Negro and white churches. There are class churches, although there is no formal segregation of classes within our churches. Class and color churches as such do not violate anything basic in the Christian faith. This is true as long as the segregation is purely voluntary, as long as it is the result of an inner desire on the part of the people to be with those with whom they can enjoy the most meaningful Christian fellowship and worship. Such separation, however, must be entirely free from external pressure. There must be freedom to attend or not to attend a particular church, to join or not to join it, to remain in its fellowship or to leave it. Our churches should open their doors to people of all classes and colors, simply because it is right to do so.

The preceding is far beyond the present practice of most churches. It is not, however, beyond the ideals the churches preach. Those ideals or standards are very high. They are ideals of perfection. It is the responsibility of our churches to preach and teach those ideals or standards undiluted. Churches face, however, some very real problems when they seek to apply those ideals of perfection to the social order and even within their own ranks. Our churches are not ideal institutions. They are composed of imperfect people. Furthermore, they are in an evil world. The question arises: What are churches to do in such an imperfect situation? There is the ideal on the one hand, and the very real situation on the other hand. There are areas and places where it seems impractical if not impossible to apply the ideal to the total and immediate situation.

Sometimes conscientious Christians are convinced that to attempt to apply fully the Christian ideal immediately even within the Christian fellowship would do more harm than good. This might be true in some sections of our country regarding segregation and desegregation. This fact, if it be a fact, would not, however, negate the Christian ideal. It would not mean that the standards and principles of the Christian religion were impractical or irrelevant. No ideal can be set aside or abrogated merely because it is difficult or even impossible to reach. The difficulty may simply point up or underscore the depth and the seriousness of sin in our lives, in our world, and even within our churches.

What is true of our churches should be true of the individual child of God. He should not search for standards that will suit him, or that will support the practices of the society in which he lives. He should seek honestly and fearlessly for the Christian ideal as revealed in the Word of God. Once he knows what God's will or ideal is for him in any area of his life, he should attempt as best he can to conform to that ideal.

Because of the limitations of our fleshly nature, our personal attainment of the Christian ideal will always be imperfect or incomplete. The fact that it is difficult and even impossible for us to attain the ideal should never lead us to tone down the ideal. We should keep it clearly in mind, and should let it continually stand in judgment against our imperfect approximation of the ideal.

There is no place right now where it seems more difficult for the child of God to measure up to the high demands of the Christian religion than in the area of race relations. In some communities the pressure on the Christian is terrific. This is particularly true of many ministers who find themselves in a frustrating dilemma. They have a deep inner desire to proclaim what they interpret to be the Word of God concerning segregation and desegregation. On the other hand, the climate in the community and even within their churches is such that they are uncertain about the effects of the proclamation of the truth. Would it do more immediate harm than good? Such ministers are caught in the typical tension of a prophet of God. They and they alone can and must decide when and what they speak. This much we can say: If they are true prophets of God, they will speak the word the Lord delivers to them. They may be convinced that God would have them be careful and tactful, but they are unworthy of the name "prophet" if they refuse to speak because they are afraid.

It may be wise for all of us to recognize that we have a prophetic ministry to perform. In Protestantism the minister is not the only prophet of God. There should be at least enough of the prophetic spirit in the pew to defend the right of God's minister to speak the word that God has delivered to him. Laymen should recognize that God's minister or prophet is responsible primarily to God and not to his congregation and certainly not to the world. Even when they do not entirely agree with him, they should defend his right to say what he interprets to be the will and purpose of God on segregation and desegregation, as on other moral issues.

There is also needed a spirit of genuine understanding by those who differ regarding segregation and desegregation. This one issue, as important as it is, should not be permitted to become a test of fellowship within our churches. There should be a searching for additional light by all concerned, by desegregationists as well as segregationists. If this additional light is to be found, freedom of discussion, private and public, must be maintained. There must not be pressure toward conformity, except the pressure that comes from truth itself.

Finally, all of us should recognize that God has a will concerning segregation and desegregation, and that his will ultimately will be done. That kind of faith can and will give to us the peace that passeth understanding, even in the midst of conflict and tension. Our faith is not centered primarily in our own efforts or in the efforts of others but in the purposes of God.

Do you remember the familiar story about President Lincoln? A minister in a delegation that visited with him said that he hoped the Lord was "on our side." The President said, "I don't agree with you." The group was amazed. The President continued, "I am not at all concerned about that, for we know that the Lord is always on the side of the right. But it is my constant anxiety and prayer that I and this nation should be on the Lord's side."

It should be our "constant anxiety and prayer" that we and our churches "should be on the Lord's side" in the present racial controversy.

APPENDIX A

United States Supreme Court Decision[1] (May 17, 1954)

Mr. Chief Justice WARREN delivered the opinion of the Court:

These cases come to us from the States of Kansas, South Carolina, Virginia, and Delaware. They are premised on different facts and different local conditions, but a common legal question justifies their consideration together in this consolidated opinion.

In each of the cases, minors of the Negro race, through their legal representatives, seek the aid of the courts in obtaining admission to the public schools of their community on a non-segregated basis. In each instance, they have been denied admission to schools attended by white children under laws requiring or permitting segregation according to race. This segregation was alleged to deprive the plaintiffs of equal protection of the laws under the Fourteenth Amendment. In each of the cases other than the Delaware case, a three-judge federal district court denied relief to the plaintiffs on the so-called "separate but equal" doctrine announced by this Court in Plessy v. Ferguson, 163 U.S. 537, 16 S.Ct. 1138, 41 L.Ed. 256. Under that doctrine, equality of treatment is accorded when the races are provided substantially equal facilities, even though these facilities be separate. In the Delaware case, the Supreme Court of Delaware adhered to that doctrine, but ordered that the plaintiffs be admitted to the white schools because of their superiority to the Negro schools.

The plaintiffs contend that segregated public schools are not "equal"

[1] The original opinion of the court included rather elaborate footnotes. These are given in full, with the complete text of the decision, in *Race Relations Law Reporter* for February, 1956, pp. 5–10.

and cannot be made "equal," and that hence they are deprived of the equal protection of the laws. Because of the obvious importance of the question presented, the Court took jurisdiction. Argument was heard in the 1952 Term, and reargument was heard this Term on certain questions propounded by the Court.

Reargument was largely devoted to the circumstances surrounding the adoption of the Fourteenth Amendment in 1868. It covered exhaustively consideration of the Amendment in Congress, ratification by the states, then existing practices in racial segregation, and the views of proponents and opponents of the Amendment. This discussion and our own investigation convince us that, although these sources cast some light, it is not enough to resolve the problem with which we are faced. At best, they are inconclusive. The most avid proponents of the post-War Amendments undoubtedly intended them to remove all legal distinctions among "all persons born or naturalized in the United States." Their opponents, just as certainly, were antagonistic to both the letter and the spirit of the Amendments and wished them to have the most limited effect. What others in Congress and the state legislatures had in mind cannot be determined with any degree of certainty.

An additional reason for the inconclusive nature of the Amendment's history, with respect to segregated schools, is the status of public education at that time. In the South, the movement toward free common schools, supported by general taxation, had not yet taken hold. Education of white children was largely in the hands of private groups. Education of Negroes was almost nonexistent, and practically all of the race were illiterate. In fact, any education of Negroes was forbidden by law in some states. Today, in contrast, many Negroes have achieved outstanding success in the arts and sciences as well as in the business and professional world. It is true that public school education at the time of the Amendment had advanced further in the North, but the effect of the Amendment on Northern States was generally ignored in the congressional debates. Even in the North, the conditions of public education did not approximate those existing today. The curriculum was usually rudimentary; ungraded schools were common in rural areas; the school term was but three months a year in many states; and compulsory school attendance was virtually unknown. As a consequence, it is not surprising that there should be so little in the history of the Fourteenth Amendment relating to its intended effect on public education.

In the first cases in this Court construing the Fourteenth Amendment, decided shortly after its adoption, the Court interpreted it as proscribing all state-imposed discriminations against the Negro race. The doctrine of "separate but equal" did not make its appearance in this Court until 1896 in the case of Plessy v. Ferguson, supra, involving not education but transportation. American courts have since labored with the doctrine for over half a century. In this Court, there have been six cases involving the "separate but equal" doctrine in the field of public education. In Cumming v. Board of Education of Richmond County, 175 U.S. 528, 20 S.Ct. 197, 44 L.Ed. 262, and Gong Lum v. Rice, 275 U.S. 78, 48 S.Ct. 91, 72 L.Ed. 172, the validity of the doctrine itself was not challenged. In more recent cases, all on the graduate school level, inequality was found in that specific benefits enjoyed by white students were denied to Negro students of the same educational qualifications. State of Missouri ex rel. Gaines v. Canada, 305 U.S. 337, 59 S.Ct. 232, 83 L.Ed. 208; Sipuel v. Board of Regents of University of Oklahoma, 332 U.S. 631, 68 S.Ct. 299, 92 L.Ed. 247; Sweatt v. Painter, 339 U.S. 629, 70 S.Ct. 848, 94 L.Ed. 1114; McLaurin v. Oklahoma State Regents, 339 U.S. 637, 70 S.Ct. 851, 94 L.Ed. 1149. In none of these cases was it necessary to re-examine the doctrine to grant relief to the Negro plaintiff. And in Sweatt v. Painter, supra, the Court expressly reserved decision on the question whether Plessy v. Ferguson should be held inapplicable to public education.

In the instant cases, that question is directly presented. Here, unlike Sweatt v. Painter, there are findings below that the Negro and white schools involved have been equalized, or are being equalized, with respect to buildings, curricula, qualifications and salaries of teachers, and other "tangible" factors. Our decision, therefore, cannot turn on merely a comparison of these tangible factors in the Negro and white schools involved in each of the cases. We must look instead to the effect of segregation itself on public education.

In approaching this problem, we cannot turn the clock back to 1868 when the Amendment was adopted, or even to 1896 when Plessy v. Ferguson was written. We must consider public education in the light of its full development and its present place in American life throughout the Nation. Only in this way can it be determined if segregation in public schools deprives these plaintiffs of the equal protection of the laws.

Today, education is perhaps the most important function of state and local governments. Compulsory school attendance laws and the great expenditures for education both demonstrate our recognition of the importance of education to our democratic society. It is required in the performance of our most basic public responsibilities, even service in the armed forces. It is the very foundation of good citizenship. Today it is a principal instrument in awakening the child to cultural values, in preparing him for later professional training, and in helping him to adjust normally to his environment. In these days, it is doubtful that any child may reasonably be expected to succeed in life if he is denied the opportunity of an education. Such an opportunity, where the state has undertaken to provide it, is a right which must be made available to all on equal terms.

We come then to the question presented: Does segregation of children in public schools solely on the basis of race, even though the physical facilities and other "tangible" factors may be equal, deprive the children of the minority group of equal educational opportunities? We believe that it does.

In Sweatt v. Painter, supra, [339 U.S. 629, 70 S.Ct. 850], in finding that a segregated law school for Negroes could not provide them equal educational opportunities, this Court relied in large part on "those qualities which are incapable of objective measurement but which make for greatness in a law school." In McLaurin v. Oklahoma State Regents, supra [339 U.S. 637, 70 S.Ct. 853], the Court, in requiring that a Negro admitted to a white graduate school be treated like all other students, again resorted to intangible considerations: ". . . his ability to study, to engage in discussions and exchange views with other students, and, in general, to learn his profession." Such considerations apply with added force to children in grade and high schools. To separate them from others of similar age and qualifications solely because of their race generates a feeling of inferiority as to their status in the community that may affect their hearts and minds in a way unlikely ever to be undone. The effect of this separation on their educational opportunities was well stated by a finding in the Kansas case by a court which nevertheless felt compelled to rule against the Negro plaintiffs:

Segregation of white and colored children in public schools has a detrimental effect upon the colored children. The impact is greater when it has the sanction of the law; for the policy of separating the races is usually interpreted as denoting the inferiority of the Negro group. A sense of inferiority affects the motivation of the child to learn. Segregation with the sanction of law, therefore, has a tendency to [retard] the educational and mental development of Negro children and to deprive them of some of the benefits they would receive in a racial [ly] integrated school system.

Whatever may have been the extent of psychological knowledge at the time of Plessy v. Ferguson, this finding is amply supported by modern authority. Any language in Plessy v. Ferguson contrary to this finding is rejected.

We conclude that in the field of public education the doctrine of "separate but equal" has no place. Separate educational facilities are inherently unequal. Therefore, we hold that the plaintiffs and others similarly situated for whom the actions have been brought are, by reason of the segregation complained of, deprived of the equal protection of the laws guaranteed by the Fourteenth Amendment. This disposition makes unnecessary any discussion whether such segregation also violates the Due Process Clause of the Fourteenth Amendment.

Because these are class actions, because of the wide applicability of this decision, and because of the great variety of local conditions, the formulation of decrees in these cases presents problems of considerable complexity. On reargument, the consideration of appropriate relief was necessarily subordinated to the primary question—the constitutionality of segregation in public education. We have now announced that such segregation is a denial of the equal protection of the laws. In order that we may have the full assistance of the parties in formulating decrees, the cases will be restored to the docket, and the parties are requested to present further argument on Questions 4 and 5 previously propounded by the Court for the reargument this Term. The Attorney General of the United States is again invited to participate. The Attorneys General of the states requiring or permitting segregation in public education will also be permitted to appear as *amici curiae* upon request to do so by September 15, 1954, and submission of briefs by October 1, 1954.

It is so ordered.

APPENDIX B

United States Supreme Court Action (May 31, 1955)

Mr. Chief Justice WARREN delivered the opinion of the Court:

These cases were decided on May 17, 1954. The opinions of that date declaring the fundamental principle that racial discrimination in public education is unconstitutional, are incorporated herein by reference. All provisions of federal, state, or local law requiring or permitting such discrimination must yield to this principle. There remains for consideration the manner in which relief is to be accorded.

Because these cases arose under different local conditions and their disposition will involve a variety of local problems, we requested further argument on the question of relief. In view of the nationwide importance of the decision, we invited the Attorney General of the United States and the Attorneys General of all states requiring or permitting racial discrimination in public education to present their views on that question. The parties, the United States, and the States of Florida, North Carolina, Arkansas, Oklahoma, Maryland, and Texas filed briefs and participated in the oral argument.

These presentations were informative and helpful to the Court in its consideration of the complexities arising from the transition to a system of public education freed of racial discrimination. The presentations also demonstrated that substantial steps to eliminate racial discrimination in public schools have already been taken, not only in some of the communities in which these cases arose, but in some of the states appearing as *amici curiae*, and in other states as well. Substantial progress has been made in the District of Columbia and in the communities in Kansas and Delaware involved in this litigation. The defendants in the cases coming to us from South Carolina and Virginia are awaiting the decision of this Court concerning relief.

Full implementation of these constitutional principles may require solution of varied local school problems. School authorities have the primary responsibility for elucidating, assessing, and solving these problems; courts will have to consider whether the action of school authorities constitutes good faith implementation of the governing constitutional principles. Because of their proximity to local conditions and the possible need for further hearings, the courts which originally heard these cases can best perform this judicial appraisal. Accordingly, we believe it appropriate to remand the cases to those courts.

In fashioning and effectuating the decrees, the courts will be guided by equitable principles. Traditionally, equity has been characterized by a practical flexibility in shaping its remedies and by a facility for adjusting and reconciling public and private needs. These cases call for the exercise of these traditional attributes of equity power. At stake is the personal interest of the plaintiffs in admission to public schools as soon as practicable on a nondiscriminatory basis. To effectuate this interest may call for elimination of a variety of obstacles in making the transition to school systems operated in accordance with the constitutional principles set forth in our May 17, 1954, decision. Courts of equity may properly take into account the public interest in the elimination of such obstacles in a systematic and effective manner. But it should go without saying that the vitality of these constitutional principles cannot be allowed to yield simply because of disagreement with them.

While giving weight to these public and private considerations, the courts will require that the defendants make a prompt and reasonable start toward full compliance with our May 17, 1954, ruling. Once such a start has been made, the courts may find that additional time is necessary to carry out the ruling in an effective manner. The burden rests upon the defendants to establish that such time is necessary in the public interest and is consistent with good faith compliance at the earliest practicable date. To that end, the courts may consider problems related to administration, arising from the physical condition of the school plant, the school transportation system, personnel, revision of school districts and attendance areas into compact units to achieve a system of determining admission to the public schools on a nonracial basis, and revision of local laws and regulations which may be necessary in solving the foregoing problems. They will also consider the adequacy of any plans the defendants may propose to meet these problems and to effectuate a transition to a racially nondiscriminatory school system. During this period of transition, the courts will retain jurisdiction of these cases.

The judgments below, except that in the Delaware case, are accordingly reversed and the cases are remanded to the District Courts to take such proceedings and enter such orders and decrees consistent with this opinion as are necessary and proper to admit to public schools on a racially nondiscriminatory basis with all deliberate speed the parties to these cases. The judgment in the Delaware case—ordering the immediate admission of the plaintiffs to schools previously attended only by white children—is affirmed on the basis of the principles stated in our May 17, 1954, opinion, but the case is remanded to the Supreme Court of Delaware for such further proceedings as that Court may deem necessary in light of this opinion.

It is so ordered.

Reading List

There are a number of books on the world-wide aspects of the race problem, such as Andrew W. Lind (ed.), *Race Relations in World Perspective* (University of Hawaii Press, 1955), consisting of papers read at the conference on Race Relations in World Perspective; Ben J. Marais, *Colour: Unsolved Problem of the West* (Howard B. Timmins, n.d.), from the viewpoint of a South African; M. F. Ashley Montagu, *Man's Most Dangerous Myth* (3rd ed.; Harper, 1952), anthropological in emphasis; Edmund D. Soper, *Racism: A World Issue* (Abingdon-Cokesbury, 1947), a standard book; and Paul A. F. Walter, Jr., *Race and Culture Relations* (McGraw-Hill, 1952), a sociological approach.

The race problem, past and present, in the United States is discussed very adequately in many books. One of the most acceptable is Arnold Rose, *The Negro in America* (Harper, 1948), which has been issued recently by Beacon Press in a paperback edition (1956) and which is a condensation of Gunnar Myrdal's *An American Dilemma*. A recent book of high quality is Stewart G. Cole and Mildren Wiese Cole, *Minorities and the American Promise* (Harper, 1954), with the subtitle "The Conflict of Principle and Practice."

There have been a number of recent books that have reported developments regarding segregation and desegregation in the South. Among them are: Wilma Dykeman and James Stokely, *Neither Black Nor White* (Rinehart, 1957), a report of a pilgrimage through the South by a Tennessee husband-and-wife writing team; John Bartlow Martin, *The Deep South Says Never* (Ballantine, 1957), a record of investigation in South Carolina, Georgia, Alabama, and Mississippi; Carl T. Rowan, *Go South to Sorrow* (Random House, 1957), a rather pessimistic picture by a Negro newspaperman; Don Shoemaker (ed.), *With All Deliberate Speed* (Harper, 1957), factual and analytical reports on segregation and desegregation in the South; and Robert Root, *Progress Against Prejudice* (Friendship Press, 1957), largely reports on progress in religious circles.

There have been a few recent books that place major emphasis on an analysis of the Southern scene. That is true of Harry S. Ashmore's *An*

176

Epitaph for Dixie (Norton, 1957, 1958), by the executive editor of the *Arkansas Gazette;* of Robert Penn Warren's brief book entitled *Segregation* (Random House, 1956); and particularly of James McBride Dabbs' *The Southern Heritage* (Knopf, 1958).

A few books are available on the educational aspects of desegregation. Two books that resulted from the same research and were both released about the time of the Supreme Court's decision are: Harry S. Ashmore, *The Negro and the Schools,* and Robin M. Williams and Margaret W. Ryan (eds.), *Schools in Transition,* both published by the University of North Carolina Press, 1954. A book covering many aspects of biracial education is Truman M. Pierce, *et al., White and Negro Schools in the South* (Prentice-Hall, 1955). Omer Carmichael and Weldon James tell *The Louisville Story* (Simon & Schuster, 1957).

There have been comparatively few books written on the contemporary racial situation from the strictly Christian viewpoint. Among those few are: Robert R. Brown, *Bigger Than Little Rock* (Seabury, 1958), largely the story of the churches and ministers of Little Rock by the Episcopal Bishop of Arkansas; John La Farge, *No Postponement* (Longmans, Green, 1950), a Roman Catholic approach and appraisal; T. B. Maston, *The Bible and Race* (Broadman, 1959), an exposition of pertinent scriptures; Liston Pope, *The Kingdom Beyond Caste* (Friendship Press, 1957), by the Southern-born dean of Yale Divinity School; Everett Tilson, *Segregation and the Bible* (Abingdon, 1958), which examines biblically based arguments of segregationists and desegregationists.

The following are a few of the books, published in recent years, that touch on various aspects of the contemporary racial situation: Charles Abrams, *Forbidden Neighbors* (Harper, 1955), "A Story of Prejudice in Housing"; Albert Blaustein and Clarence Clyde Ferguson, Jr., *Desegregation and the Law* (Rutgers University Press, 1957); Margaret Just Butcher, *The Negro in American Culture* (Knopf, 1956); George W. Cable, *The Negro Question,* edited by Arlin Turner (Doubleday, 1958), selected writing on civil rights by Cable—remarkably relevant though written in the 1880's and 1890's; E. Franklin Frazier, *Black Bourgeoisie* (Free Press, 1957), an analysis by a Negro scholar; J. G. Furnas, *Goodbye to Uncle Tom* (William Sloane Associates, 1956); Warrent D. St. James, *The National Association for the Advancement of Colored People* (Exposition Press, 1958), a carefully documented story. Other books that will be of interest to some are *How Far the Promised Land?* (Viking Press, 1955) by Walter White, who was executive secretary of the National Association for the Advancement of Colored People from 1918 until his death in 1955, and *The Strange Career of Jim Crow* (Oxford

University Press, 1955) by C. Vann Woodward, a series of lectures by a scholar to a university audience but readable in style and eminently worth reading.

For those who want to keep up with current developments particularly in the area of desegregation, there are the *Southern School News*, a monthly publication of the Southern Education Reporting Service, P.O. Box 6156, Acklen Station, Nashville 5, Tennessee; and *Race Relations Law Reporter*, published six times a year by the Vanderbilt University School of Law, Nashville 5, Tennessee.